Competent National Authorities under the International Drug Control Treaties

With introductory texts in Arabic, Chinese and Russian

Autorités nationales compétentes au titre des traités internationaux concernant le contrôle des drogues

Avec une introduction en arabe, en chinois et en russe

Organismos nacionales competentes en virtud de los tratados internacionales de fiscalización de drogas

Con introducciones en árabe, chino y ruso

UNITED NATIONS — NATIONS UNIES — NACIONES UNIDAS
New York, 2016

Note

Symbols of United Nations documents are composed of capital letters combined with figures. Mention of such symbols indicates a reference to a United Nations document.

ST/NAR.3/2015/1(E/NA)

UNITED NATIONS PUBLICATION
Sales No. T.16.XI.5
ISBN: 978-92-1-048162-5
eISBN: 978-92-1-057764-9
ISSN: 0251-6799

This publication has not been formally edited.

Publishing production: English, Publishing and Library Section, United Nations Office at Vienna.

CONTENTS

TABLE DES MATIÈRES

ÍNDICE

СОДЕРЖАНИЕ

目录

المحتويات

PREFACE

The present directory lists titles and addresses of the following:

(a) Competent national authorities empowered to issue certificates and authorizations for the import and export of narcotic drugs and psychotropic substances in accordance with the provisions of article 18 of the Single Convention on Narcotic Drugs of 1961 and article 16 of the Convention on Psychotropic Substances of 1971;

(b) Competent national authorities empowered to regulate or enforce national controls over precursors and essential chemicals in accordance with the provisions of article 12 of the United Nations Convention against Illicit Traffic in Narcotic Drugs and Psychotropic Substances of 1988;

(c) Competent international bodies that might assist national competent authorities in case no national authority is listed for a given country or area or in case contact cannot be established with the listed authorities.

The directory, which is issued annually, also includes the telephone and telefacsimile numbers and e-mail addresses, if available, of the national authorities or international bodies in question.

The titles and addresses of the national authorities are given in English, French and Spanish and are listed in English alphabetical order under the countries and areas that they serve. For ease of reference, there are indexes of the names of the countries and areas in English, French and Spanish. Names and addresses of competent international bodies that might serve as a gateway to communicating with Governments appear in English alphabetical order. For ease of reference, the names of those international bodies are included at the end of the English, French and Spanish indexes.

The designations employed and the presentation of material do not imply the expression of any opinion on the part of the Secretariat of the United Nations concerning the legal status of any country, territory, city or area, or any authority, or concerning the delimitation of any frontiers or boundaries.

Italics are used to indicate areas other than countries (such as territories).

Governments are requested to review the information in the present directory and to communicate any changes to the United Nations Office on Drugs and Crime.

PRÉFACE

Le présent document contient une liste des titres et adresses:

a) Des autorités nationales habilitées à délivrer des certificats et des autorisations pour l'importation et l'exportation de stupéfiants et de substances psychotropes, conformément aux dispositions de l'article 18 de la Convention unique sur les stupéfiants de 1961 et de l'article 16 de la Convention de 1971 sur les substances psychotropes;

b) Des autorités nationales habilitées à réglementer les précurseurs et les produits chimiques essentiels ou à leur appliquer des mesures de contrôle national, conformément aux dispositions de l'article 12 de la Convention des Nations Unies contre le trafic illicite de stupéfiants et de substances psychotropes de 1988;

c) Des organismes internationaux compétents qui peuvent aider les autorités des pays, territoires ou zones pour lesquels aucune autorité nationale n'est indiquée ou avec lesquels aucun contact ne peut être établi.

Cette liste, qui est publiée chaque année, contient également les numéros de téléphone et de télécopieur ainsi que les adresses électroniques, le cas échéant, des autorités nationales ou des organismes internationaux en question.

Les titres et adresses des autorités nationales sont donnés en anglais, espagnol et français, et sont présentés dans l'ordre alphabétique anglais sous le nom des pays, territoires et zones dont ils relèvent. Pour faciliter les recherches, la liste contient des index des pays, territoires et zones en anglais, espagnol et français. Les noms et adresses des organismes internationaux compétents qui seraient en mesure d'établir des contacts avec les gouvernements figurent dans l'ordre alphabétique anglais. Pour faciliter les recherches, les noms de ces organismes internationaux sont donnés à la fin des index anglais, espagnol et français.

Les appellations employées et la présentation des données n'impliquent de la part du Secrétariat de l'Organisation des Nations Unies aucune prise de position quant au statut juridique des pays, territoires, villes ou zones, ou de leurs autorités, ni quant au tracé de leurs frontières ou limites.

Les zones autres que des pays (par exemple des territoires) sont indiquées en italique.

Les gouvernements sont invités à vérifier les informations figurant dans le présent répertoire et à communiquer toute modification à l'Office des Nations Unies contre la drogue et le crime.

PREFACIO

En la presente guía figuran los nombres y las direcciones de:

a) Los organismos nacionales competentes que están facultados para emitir certificados y autorizaciones de importación y exportación de estupefacientes y sustancias sicotrópicas de conformidad con lo dispuesto en el artículo 18 de la Convención Única de 1961 sobre Estupefacientes y en el artículo 16 del Convenio sobre Sustancias Sicotrópicas de 1971;

b) Los organismos nacionales competentes que están facultados para establecer o hacer cumplir normas nacionales para la fiscalización de precursores y de productos químicos esenciales de conformidad con lo dispuesto en el artículo 12 de la Convención de las Naciones Unidas contra el Tráfico Ilícito de Estupefacientes y Sustancias Sicotrópicas de 1988;

c) Los órganos internacionales competentes que podrían ayudar a los organismos nacionales competentes en caso de que no se indique ningún organismo nacional de un determinado país, territorio o zona o en caso de que no pueda establecerse contacto con los organismos indicados.

Esta guía, que se publica anualmente, incluye también los números de teléfono y de telefax, así como las direcciones de correo electrónico disponibles, de los organismos nacionales o los órganos internacionales en cuestión.

Los nombres y direcciones de los organismos nacionales figuran en español, francés e inglés y se enumeran siguiendo el orden alfabético en inglés de los países, territorios y zonas en que prestan servicios. Para facilitar las consultas, se han incluido índices de los nombres de los países, territorios y zonas en español, francés e inglés. Los nombres y direcciones de los órganos internacionales competentes que podrían servir para ponerse en comunicación con los gobiernos aparecen en orden alfabético inglés. Para facilitar las consultas, los nombres de esos órganos internacionales se incluyen al final de los índices español, francés e inglés.

Las denominaciones empleadas en esta publicación y la forma en que aparecen presentados los datos que contiene no entrañan, de parte de la Secretaría de las Naciones Unidas, juicio alguno sobre la condición jurídica de ninguno de los países o territorios citados o de sus autoridades, ni respecto de la delimitación de sus fronteras o límites.

Las zonas que no son países (como los territorios) van en cursiva.

Se ruega a los gobiernos que examinen la información que figura en la presente guía y que comuniquen cualquier cambio a la Oficina de las Naciones Unidas contra la Droga y el Delito.

ПРЕДИСЛОВИЕ

Настоящий справочник содержит названия и адреса:

a) компетентных национальных органов, уполномоченных выдавать свидетельства и разрешения на ввоз и вывоз наркотических средств и психотропных веществ в соответствии с положениями статьи 18 Единой конвенции о наркотических средствах 1961 года и статьи 16 Конвенции о психотропных веществах 1971 года;

b) компетентных национальных органов, уполномоченных осуществлять регулирование или обеспечивать соблюдение национальных мер по контролю над прекурсорами и основными химическими веществами в соответствии с положениями статьи 12 Конвенции Организации Объединенных Наций о борьбе против незаконного оборота наркотических средств и психотропных веществ 1988 года;

c) компетентных международных органов, которые могут содействовать компетентным национальным органам в случаях, когда не указаны национальные органы по какой-либо стране или району или когда с указанными органами не может быть установлен контакт.

В этом ежегодно издаваемом справочнике указываются также номера телефонов и факсимильной связи и адреса электронной почты соответствующих национальных или международных органов, если таковые имеются.

Названия и адреса национальных органов приводятся на английском, французском и испанском языках с перечислением обслуживаемых ими стран и районов в английском алфавитном порядке. Для облегчения работы с документом к нему прилагается указатель названий стран и районов на английском, французском и испанском языках. Названия и адреса компетентных международных органов, которые могут содействовать установлению связи с правительствами, приводятся в английском алфавитном порядке. Для облегчения работы с документом названия таких международных органов перечислены в конце указателей на английском, французском и испанском языках.

Употребляемые обозначения и изложение материала не означают выражения со стороны Секретариата Организации Объединенных Наций какого бы то ни было мнения относительно правового статуса страны, территории, города или района, или каких-либо властей, или относительно делимитации их границ.

Курсивом выделены районы, отличные от стран (например, территории).

Правительствам предлагается рассмотреть информацию, содержащуюся в настоящем справочнике, и направить сообщения о любых изменениях Управлению Организации Объединенных Наций по наркотикам и преступности.

序言

本名录列有下列主管部门的名称和地址：

(a) 负责根据 1961 年《麻醉品单一公约》第 18 条和 1971 年《精神药物公约》第 16 条规定签发麻醉药品和精神药物进出口证书和准许证的国家主管部门；

(b) 负责根据 1988 年《联合国禁止非法贩运麻醉药品和精神药物公约》第 12 条规定对前体和基本化学品实行监管或国家管制的国家主管部门；

(c) 在某一国家或地区未列有国家部门或无法与所列部门取得联系的情况下可对国家主管部门给予协助的国际主管机构。

本名录每年发布一次，其中还载列有关国家部门或国际机构的电话和传真号码，如有电子邮箱地址，也包括在内。

国家主管部门的名称和地址以英文、法文和西班牙文列出，按所属国家和地区的英文字母顺序排列。为便于查阅，附有国家和地区的英文、法文和西班牙文名称索引。一些国际主管机构可作为与政府进行联系的中间途径，这些机构的名称和地址按英文字母顺序列出。为便于查阅，这些国际机构的名称列在英文、法文和西班牙文索引之后。

所使用的名称和材料编排方式并不意味着联合国秘书处对任何国家、领土、城市或地区或任何当局的法律地位，或者对其任何边界和界线的划分表示任何意见。

斜体用以表示除国家之外的地区（例如属地）。

请各国政府审查本名录所载资料，如有改动，请通知联合国毒品和犯罪问题办公室。

تصدير

يتضمّن هذا الدليل قائمة بأسماء وعناوين السلطات التالية:

(أ) السلطات الوطنية المختصة المخوّلة إصدار شهادات وأذون استيراد وتصدير المخدرات والمؤثرات العقلية، وفقا لأحكام المادة ١٨ من الاتفاقية الوحيدة للمخدرات لسنة ١٩٦١، والمادة ١٦ من اتفاقية المؤثرات العقلية لسنة ١٩٧١؛

(ب) السلطات الوطنية المختصة المخوّلة تنظيم أو إنفاذ الضوابط الوطنية المفروضة على السلائف والكيماويات الأساسية وفقا لأحكام المادة ١٢ من اتفاقية الأمم المتحدة لمكافحة الاتجار غير المشروع في المخدرات والمؤثرات العقلية لسنة ١٩٨٨؛

(ج) الهيئات الدولية المختصة التي يمكن أن تساعد السلطات الوطنية المختصة في حال عدم إدراج اسم سلطة وطنية لبلد أو إقليم معيّن، أو في حال تعذر إقامة اتصال بالسلطات المدرجة في القائمة.

وهذا الدليل، الذي يصدر سنويا، يتضمن أيضا أرقام الهاتف والفاكس وعناوين البريد الإلكتروني، إن وجدت، الخاصة بالسلطات الوطنية أو الهيئات الدولية المعنية.

وترد أسماء وعناوين تلك السلطات الوطنية باللغات الإسبانية والإنكليزية والفرنسية، وبالترتيب الأبجدي الإنكليزي، تحت أسماء ما تتبعه من دول وأقاليم. ولتسهيل الرجوع إلى المعلومات المطلوبة، تم عمل فهارس بأسماء الدول والأقاليم باللغات الإسبانية والإنكليزية والفرنسية. أما أسماء وعناوين الهيئة الدولية المختصة التي قد تتخذ كقناة للاتصال بالحكومات فترد بالترتيب الأبجدي الإنكليزي في نهاية الجزء الذي تتعلق به. وتسهيلا للرجوع، أُدرجت أسماء تلك الهيئات الدولية في نهاية الفهارس الإسبانية والإنكليزية والفرنسية.

ولا تنطوي التسميات المستخدمة ولا طريقة عرض المادة على الإعراب عن أي رأي كان من جانب الأمانة العامة للأمم المتحدة بشأن المركز القانوني لأي بلد أو إقليم أو مدينة أو منطقة، أو لأية سلطة، أو بشأن تعيين أي حدود أو تخوم.

وتستخدم الكتابة المائلة للدلالة على المناطق التي ليست بلدانا (مثل الأقاليم).

ويرجى من الحكومات مراجعة المعلومات الواردة في هذا الدليل وإبلاغ مكتب الأمم المتحدة المعني بالمخدرات والجريمة بأية تغييرات تدخل عليها.

Competent national authorities under article 18 of the Single Convention on Narcotic Drugs of 1961 and article 16 of the Convention on Psychotropic Substances of 1971

The present directory lists all competent national authorities empowered to issue certificates and authorizations for the import and export of narcotic drugs and psychotropic substances in accordance with the provisions of article 18 of the Single Convention on Narcotic Drugs of 1961 and article 16 of the Convention on Psychotropic Substances of 1971.

This listing of national authorities is issued pursuant to the 1961 Convention and the 1971 Convention. It follows the practice established following the entry into force of the 1931 Convention for Limiting and Regulating the Distribution of Narcotic Drugs, which was brought under the aegis of the United Nations by the 1946 Protocol amending the latter convention. Its contents are based on data provided to the Secretary-General in the annual reports on the working of the international drug control treaties by States both parties and non-parties to the relevant treaties.

Authorities indicated in this directory under article 18 are empowered to issue import and export authorizations only for narcotic drugs.

Authorities indicated in this directory under article 16 are empowered to issue import and export authorizations only for psychotropic substances.

Authorities indicated in this directory under articles 18 and 16 are empowered to issue import and export authorizations for both narcotic drugs and psychotropic substances.

The absence of a reference to an article of these conventions before the name of an authority in this directory indicates that the Government has not specified the range of empowerment of this respective authority.

If a contact address for a country or area is not listed under the competent national authorities under article 18 of the Single Convention on Narcotic Drugs of 1961 and article 16 of the Convention on Psychotropic Substances of 1971 of the present publication, it is possible that there is a contact address for that country or area listed under the competent national authorities under article 12 of the United Nations Convention against Illicit Traffic in Narcotic Drugs and Psychotropic Substances of 1988 that may be used.

Governments are requested to review the information in this directory and to communicate any changes with regard to article 18 of the Single Convention on Narcotic Drugs of 1961 and article 16 of the Convention on Psychotropic Substances of 1971 to the United Nations Office on Drugs and Crime, Secretariat to the Governing Bodies, Vienna International Centre, P.O. Box 500, 1400 Vienna, Austria (Fax: (+43-1) 26060-5885; E-mail: sgb@unodc.org).

Competent national authorities under article 12 of the United Nations Convention against Illicit Traffic in Narcotic Drugs and Psychotropic Substances of 1988

The present directory also lists all competent national authorities empowered to regulate or enforce national controls over precursors and essential chemicals in accordance with the provisions of article 12 of the United Nations Convention against Illicit Traffic in Narcotic Drugs and Psychotropic Substances of 1988.

This listing of national authorities is issued pursuant to Economic and Social Council resolution 1992/29 of 30 July 1992. Its contents are based on data provided to the International Narcotics Control Board (INCB) by Governments.

Notes verbales were transmitted by the Secretary-General to all States requesting names and addresses of competent national authorities empowered to implement the provisions of article 12 of the 1988 Convention. The national authorities that were identified by Governments in reply to those notes verbales appear in the list below without an asterisk. Authorities marked with an asterisk (*) are those competent national authorities currently reporting to INCB under the provisions of article 12, paragraph 12, of the 1988 Convention but which were not expressly identified by Governments in reply to the notes verbales.

If a contact address for a country or area is not listed under article 12 of the United Nations Convention against Illicit Traffic in Narcotic Drugs and Psychotropic Substances of 1988 of the present publication, it is possible that there is a contact address for that country or area listed under the competent national authorities under article 18 of the Single Convention on Narcotic Drugs of 1961 and article 16 of the Convention on Psychotropic Substances of 1971 that may be used. Alternatively, the INCB secretariat or other competent international bodies may be contacted for further information. The names and addresses of those international bodies appear at the end of this directory.

Knowledge of the respective roles and responsibilities entrusted to each competent authority in relation to the implementation of specific control measures is essential if rapid and effective exchange of information between Governments is to be made possible. It should be recalled that the Economic and Social Council, in its resolution 1992/29, invited "States in which precursor and essential chemicals are manufactured and States in regions in which narcotic drugs and psychotropic substances are illicitly manufactured to establish close cooperation in order to prevent the diversion of precursor and essential chemicals into illicit channels". Furthermore, the Council urged States exporting chemicals essential to the illicit production of heroin and cocaine to ensure that the competent authorities, in considering applications for export authorizations, "take reasonable steps to verify the legitimacy of transactions, in consultation, where appropriate, with their counterparts in importing countries". Experience has shown that direct contact, where appropriate, is often the most expeditious means of identifying and stopping suspicious transactions involving scheduled substances.

Governments are requested to review the information under article 12 of the United Nations Convention against Illicit Traffic in Narcotic Drugs and Psychotropic Substances of 1988 and to communicate any changes to the United Nations Office on Drugs and Crime, Secretariat of the International Narcotics Control Board, Vienna International Centre, P.O. Box 500, 1400 Vienna, Austria (Fax: (+43-1) 26060-5867; E-mail: secretariat@incb.org).

Autorités nationales compétentes au titre de l'article 18 de la Convention unique sur les stupéfiants de 1961 et de l'article 16 de la Convention sur les substances psychotropes de 1971

Le présent répertoire contient une liste de toutes les autorités nationales habilitées à délivrer des certificats et des autorisations pour l'importation et l'exportation de stupéfiants et de substances psychotropes, conformément aux dispositions de l'article 18 de la Convention unique sur les stupéfiants de 1961 et de l'article 16 de la Convention sur les substances psychotropes de 1971.

Cette liste est publiée en application des Conventions de 1961 et de 1971, conformément à la pratique établie après l'entrée en vigueur de la Convention pour limiter la fabrication et réglementer la distribution des stupéfiants de 1931 qui a été placée sous l'égide de l'Organisation des Nations Unies par le Protocole de 1946 amendant cette dernière convention. Cette liste a été établie à partir des données communiquées au Secrétaire général dans les rapports annuels sur le fonctionnement des traités internationaux concernant le contrôle des drogues envoyés par les États parties ou non parties auxdits traités.

Les autorités répertoriées au titre de l'article 18 ne sont habilitées qu'à délivrer des autorisations d'importation et d'exportation pour les stupéfiants.

Les autorités répertoriées au titre de l'article 16 ne sont habilitées qu'à délivrer des autorisations d'importation et d'exportation pour les substances psychotropes.

Les autorités répertoriées au titre des articles 18 et 16 sont habilitées à délivrer des autorisations d'importation et d'exportation pour les stupéfiants et pour les substances psychotropes.

L'absence de référence à un article de ces conventions avant le nom d'une autorité figurant dans ce répertoire signifie que le gouvernement n'a pas précisé le mandat de l'autorité en question.

S'il n'y a pas d'adresse de contact pour un pays, territoire ou zone dans la liste des autorités nationales compétentes au titre de l'article 18 de la Convention unique sur les stupéfiants de 1961 et de l'article 16 de la Convention sur les substances psychotropes de 1971 figurant dans la présente publication, il se peut que la liste des autorités nationales compétentes au titre de l'article 12 de la Convention des Nations Unies contre le trafic illicite de stupéfiants et de substances psychotropes de 1988 contienne une adresse utilisable pour ce même pays, territoire ou zone.

Les gouvernements sont invités à vérifier les informations figurant dans le présent répertoire et à communiquer toute modification en rapport avec l'article 18 de la Convention unique sur les stupéfiants de 1961 et l'article 16 de la Convention sur les substances psychotropes de 1971 à l'Office des Nations Unies contre la drogue et le crime, Secrétariat des organes directeurs, Centre international de Vienne, B.P. 500, 1400 Vienne (Autriche) [Télécopieur: (+43-1) 26060-5885; Courriel: sgb@unodc.org].

Autorités nationales compétentes au titre de l'article 12 de la Convention des Nations Unies contre le trafic illicite de stupéfiants et de substances psychotropes de 1988

Le présent répertoire contient aussi une liste de toutes les autorités nationales habilitées à réglementer les précurseurs et les produits chimiques essentiels ou à leur appliquer des mesures de contrôle national, en application des dispositions de l'article 12 de la Convention des Nations Unies contre le trafic illicite de stupéfiants et de substances psychotropes de 1988.

Cette liste est publiée en application de la résolution 1992/29 du Conseil économique et social en date du 30 juillet 1992. Elle est fondée sur les données communiquées par les gouvernements à l'Organe international de contrôle des stupéfiants (OICS).

Le Secrétaire général a envoyé à tous les États des notes verbales pour leur demander de lui communiquer le nom et l'adresse des autorités nationales habilitées à appliquer les dispositions de l'article 12 de la Convention de 1988. Les autorités dont le nom a été donné par les gouvernements en réponse à ces notes verbales sont indiquées telles quelles. Celles dont le nom est accompagné d'un astérisque (*) sont celles qui font actuellement rapport à l'OICS, en application des dispositions du paragraphe 12 de l'article 12 de la Convention de 1988 mais qui n'ont pas été expressément citées par les gouvernements en réponse aux notes verbales.

S'il n'y a pas d'adresse pour un pays, un territoire ou une zone au titre de l'article 12 de la Convention des Nations Unies contre le trafic illicite de stupéfiants et de substances psychotropes de 1988, il se peut que la liste des autorités nationales compétentes au titre de l'article 18 de la Convention unique sur les stupéfiants de 1961 et de l'article 16 de la Convention sur les substances psychotropes de 1971 contienne une adresse utilisable pour ce même pays, territoire ou zone. Des renseignements complémentaires peuvent aussi être demandés au secrétariat de l'OICS ou à des organismes internationaux compétents dont les noms et adresses figurent à la fin du présent répertoire.

Il est indispensable de connaître le rôle et les responsabilités respectifs de chaque autorité compétente en ce qui concerne l'application de mesures spécifiques de contrôle si l'on veut obtenir un échange rapide et efficace d'informations entre les gouvernements. Il convient de rappeler que le Conseil économique et social, dans sa résolution 1992/29, a invité "les États où sont fabriqués des précurseurs et des produits chimiques essentiels, ainsi que les États des régions où des stupéfiants et des substances psychotropes sont fabriqués illicitement, à établir des liens de coopération étroits afin d'empêcher le détournement de précurseurs et produits chimiques essentiels vers des circuits illicites". Le Conseil a en outre prié instamment les États exportant des produits chimiques essentiels pour la production illicite d'héroïne et de cocaïne de veiller à ce que les autorités compétentes de ces pays, lorsqu'elles examinent les demandes d'autorisation d'exportation, "prennent toutes les mesures qui peuvent raisonnablement être prises pour vérifier la légitimité des opérations et, selon qu'il convient, se consulter avec leurs homologues des pays importateurs". L'expérience montre que des contacts directs sont souvent le moyen le plus rapide de déceler et d'arrêter des transactions suspectes portant sur des substances inscrites aux Tableaux.

Les gouvernements sont invités à vérifier les informations au titre de l'article 12 de la Convention des Nations Unies contre le trafic illicite de stupéfiants et de substances psychotropes de 1988 et à communiquer toute modification à l'Office des Nations Unies contre la drogue et le crime, Secrétariat de l'Organe international de contrôle des stupéfiants, Centre international de Vienne, B.P. 500, 1400 Vienne (Autriche) [Télécopieur: (+43-1) 26060-5867; courrier électronique: secretariat@incb.org].

Organismos nacionales competentes a los efectos del artículo 18 de la Convención Única de 1961 sobre Estupefacientes y del artículo 16 del Convenio sobre Sustancias Sicotrópicas de 1971

En la presente guía figuran todos los organismos nacionales competentes que están facultados para emitir certificados y autorizaciones de importación y exportación de estupefacientes y sustancias sicotrópicas de conformidad con lo dispuesto en el artículo 18 de la Convención Única de 1961 sobre Estupefacientes y en el artículo 16 del Convenio sobre Sustancias Sicotrópicas de 1971.

Esa lista de los organismos nacionales se publica de conformidad con la Convención de 1961 y el Convenio de 1971. Con ella se sigue el sistema establecido tras la entrada en vigor de la Convención de 1931 para limitar la fabricación y reglamentar la distribución de estupefacientes, que pasó a estar bajo la égida de las Naciones Unidas a partir de la firma del Protocolo de enmienda de 1946. Su contenido se basa en los datos proporcionados al Secretario General, en los informes anuales sobre la aplicación de los tratados internacionales de fiscalización de drogas, tanto por los Estados que son parte en los tratados pertinentes como por los que no lo son.

Los organismos indicados a los efectos del artículo 18 están facultados para emitir autorizaciones de importación y exportación de estupefacientes solamente.

Los organismos indicados a los efectos del artículo 16 están facultados para emitir atorizaciones de importación y exportación de sustancias sicotrópicas solamente.

Los organismos indicados a los efectos de los artículos 18 y 16 están facultados para emitir autorizaciones de importación y exportación tanto de sustancias sicotrópicas como de estupefacientes.

La falta de cualquiera de esas indicaciones significa que el gobierno no ha comunicado el ámbito de competencia de los organismos respectivos.

Si en las partes de la presente publicación, en el lugar en que figuran los organismos nacionales competentes a los efectos del artículo 18 de la Convención Única de 1961 sobre Estupefacientes y del artículo 16 del Convenio sobre Sustancias Sicotrópicas de 1971, no se indica ninguna dirección para ponerse en contacto con un determinado país, territorio o zona, es posible que figure alguna dirección que pueda utilizarse para ese país, territorio o zona en la parte de la publicación donde figuran los organismos nacionales competentes a los efectos del artículo 12 de la Convención de las Naciones Unidas contra el Tráfico Ilícito de Estupefacientes y Sustancias Sicotrópicas de 1988.

Se ruega a los gobiernos que examinen la información que figura en la presente guía y que comuniquen cualquier cambio con respecto al artículo 18 de la Convención Única de 1961 sobre Estupefacientes y el artículo 16 del Convenio sobre Sustancias Sicotrópicas de 1971 a la Oficina de las Naciones Unidas contra la Droga y el Delito, Secretaría de los Órganos Normativos, Vienna International Centre, P.O. Box 500, 1400 Vienna, Austria (fax: (+43-1) 26060-5885; correo electrónico: sgb@unodc.org).

Organismos nacionales competentes a los efectos del artículo 12 de la Convención de las Naciones Unidas contra el Tráfico Ilícito de Estupefacientes y Sustancias Sicotrópicas de 1988

En la presente guía figuran también todos los organismos nacionales competentes que están facultados para establecer o hacer cumplir normas nacionales para la fiscalización de precursores y de productos químicos esenciales de conformidad con lo dispuesto en el artículo 12 de la Convención de las Naciones Unidas contra el Tráfico Ilícito de Estupefacientes y Sustancias Sicotrópicas de 1988.

Esa lista de organismos nacionales se publica de conformidad con la resolución 1992/29, de 30 de julio de 1992, del Consejo Económico y Social. Su contenido se basa en los datos proporcionados por los gobiernos a la Junta Internacional de Fiscalización de Estupefacientes (JIFE).

El Secretario General envió a todos los Estados unas notas verbales en las que solicitaba los nombres y direcciones de los organismos nacionales competentes que estaban facultados para cumplir lo dispuesto en el artículo 12 de la Convención de 1988. Los organismos nacionales mencionados por los gobiernos en sus respuestas a esas notas verbales figuran en la lista sin asterisco. Los organismos señalados con un asterisco (*) son los organismos nacionales competentes que actualmente informan a la JIFE en virtud de lo dispuesto en el párrafo 12 del artículo 12 de la Convención de 1988 pero que no fueron mencionados expresamente por los gobiernos en sus respuestas a las notas verbales.

Si en la parte de la presente publicación, en el lugar en que figuran los organismos nacionales competentes a los efectos del artículo 12 de la Convención de las Naciones Unidas contra el Tráfico Ilícito de Estupefacientes y Sustancias Sicotrópicas de 1988, no se indica ninguna dirección para ponerse en contacto con un determinado país, territorio o zona, es posible que figure alguna dirección que pueda utilizarse para ese país, territorio o zona en las partes de la presente publicación donde figuran los organismos nacionales competentes a los efectos del artículo 18 de la Convención Única de 1961 sobre Estupefacientes y del artículo 16 del Convenio sobre Sustancias Sicotrópicas de 1971. O bien, para más información, pueden dirigirse a la secretaría de la JIFE o a otros órganos internacionales competentes. Los nombres y direcciones de esos órganos internacionales figuran al final de esta guía.

Es indispensable conocer las funciones y cometidos confiados a cada organismo competente en relación con la aplicación de medidas de fiscalización específicas para que sea posible un intercambio de información rápido y eficaz entre los gobiernos. Debe recordarse que el Consejo Económico y Social, en su resolución 1992/29, invitó "a los Estados que fabrican precursores y productos químicos esenciales y a los Estados de regiones en las que se fabriquen ilícitamente estupefacientes y sustancias sicotrópicas a establecer una cooperación estrecha con el fin de prevenir la desviación de precursores y de productos químicos esenciales hacia canales ilícitos". Además, el Consejo instó a los Estados exportadores de sustancias químicas esenciales para la producción ilícita de heroína y cocaína, a asegurarse de que sus organismos competentes, cuando examinen las solicitudes de autorización de exportación, "tomen todas las medidas razonables para verificar el carácter legítimo de las transacciones, en consulta, cuando proceda, con las autoridades competentes de los países de importación". La experiencia enseña que el contacto directo, cuando procede, es a menudo el medio más rápido de identificar y detener las transacciones sospechosas relativas a sustancias enumeradas en las listas.

Se ruega a los gobiernos que examinen la información que figura a los efectos del artículo 12 de la Convención de las Naciones Unidas contra el Tráfico Ilícito de Estupefacientes y Sustancias Sicotrópicas de 1988 y que comuniquen cualquier cambio a la Oficina de las Naciones Unidas contra la Droga y el Delito, Secretaría de la Junta Internacional de Fiscalización de Estupefacientes, Vienna International Centre, P.O. Box 500, 1400 Vienna, Austria (fax: (+43-1) 26060-5867; correo electrónico: secretariat@incb.org).

Компетентные национальные органы, действующие на основании положений статьи 18 Единой конвенции о наркотических средствах 1961 года и статьи 16 Конвенции о психотропных веществах 1971 года

В настоящем справочнике перечислены все компетентные национальные органы, уполномоченные выдавать свидетельства и разрешения на ввоз и вывоз наркотических средств и психотропных веществ в соответствии с положениями статьи 18 Единой конвенции о наркотических средствах 1961 года и статьи 16 Конвенции о психотропных веществах 1971 года.

Настоящий перечень национальных органов издается в соответствии с положениями Конвенций 1961 и 1971 годов. Таким образом, продолжается практика, установленная после вступления в силу Конвенции об ограничении и регламентации распределения наркотических средств 1931 года, которая в силу Протокола 1946 года о внесении поправок к данной Конвенции была включена в систему конвенций Организации Объединенных Наций. Этот перечень подготовлен на основе данных, представленных Генеральному секретарю в ежегодных докладах о применении международных договоров в области контроля над наркотиками государствами, как являющимися, так и не являющимися сторонами соответствующих договоров.

Органы, указанные в настоящем справочнике применительно к статье 18, уполномочены выдавать разрешения на ввоз и вывоз лишь наркотических средств.

Органы, указанные в настоящем справочнике применительно к статье 16, уполномочены выдавать разрешения на ввоз и вывоз лишь психотропных веществ.

Органы, указанные в настоящем справочнике применительно к статьям 18 и 16, уполномочены выдавать разрешения на ввоз и вывоз как наркотических средств, так и психотропных веществ.

Отсутствие ссылки в настоящем справочнике на какую-либо статью этих конвенций перед названием компетентного органа свидетельствует о том, что правительство не определило круг полномочий соответствующего органа.

Если контактный адрес по стране или району не включен в информацию о компетентных национальных органах, действующих на основании статьи 18 Единой конвенции о наркотических средствах 1961 года и статьи 16 Конвенции о психотропных веществах 1971 года, в настоящей публикации, то, возможно, контактный адрес по этой стране или району, которым можно воспользоваться, указан в информации о компетентных национальных органах, действующих на основании статьи 12 Конвенции Организации Объединенных Наций о борьбе против незаконного оборота наркотических средств и психотропных веществ 1988 года.

Правительствам предлагается рассмотреть информацию, содержащуюся в настоящем справочнике, и направить сообщения о любых изменениях, касающихся статьи 18 Единой конвенции о наркотических средствах 1961 года и статьи 16 Конвенции о психотропных веществах 1971 года, по адресу: United Nations Office on Drugs and Crime, Secretariat to the Governing Bodies, Vienna International Centre, P.O. Box 500, 1400 Vienna, Austria (факс: (+43-1) 26060-5885; адрес эл. почты: sgb@unodc.org).

**Компетентные национальные органы, действующие
на основании положений статьи 12 Конвенции Организации Объединенных
Наций о борьбе против незаконного оборота наркотических средств и
психотропных веществ 1988 года**

В настоящем справочнике перечислены также все компетентные национальные органы, уполномоченные осуществлять регулирование или обеспечивать соблюдение национальных мер по контролю над прекурсорами и основными химическими веществами в соответствии с положениями статьи 12 Конвенции Организации Объединенных Наций о борьбе против незаконного оборота наркотических средств и психотропных веществ 1988 года.

Настоящий перечень национальных органов издается в соответствии с резолюцией 1992/29 Экономического и Социального Совета от 30 июля 1992 года. Он готовится на основе данных, представляемых правительствами Международному комитету по контролю над наркотиками (МККН).

Всем государствам были направлены вербальные ноты Генерального секретаря, в которых содержалась просьба сообщить названия и адреса компетентных национальных органов, уполномоченных осуществлять положения статьи 12 Конвенции 1988 года. Национальные органы, указанные правительствами в ответ на эти вербальные ноты, не помечены в представленном ниже перечне звездочкой (*). С другой стороны, звездочкой (*) отмечены компетентные национальные органы, которые в настоящее время представляют МККН информацию в соответствии с положениями пункта 12 статьи 12 Конвенции 1988 года, но которые не были прямо указаны правительствами в связи с вербальными нотами Генерального секретаря.

Если контактный адрес по стране или району не включен в информацию о компетентных национальных органах, действующих на основании статьи 12 Конвенции Организации Объединенных Наций о борьбе против незаконного оборота наркотических средств и психотропных веществ 1988 года в настоящей публикации, то, возможно, контактный адрес по этой стране или району, которым можно воспользоваться, указан в информации о компетентных национальных органах, действующих на основании статьи 18 Единой конвенции о наркотических средствах 1961 года и статьи 16 Конвенции о психотропных веществах 1971 года. За дополнительной информацией можно также обратиться в секретариат МККН или в другие компетентные международные органы. Названия и адреса таких международных органов приведены в конце настоящего справочника.

Для обеспечения быстрого и эффективного обмена информацией между правительствами крайне важно располагать данными о соответствующих функциях и обязанностях каждого компетентного органа в связи с осуществлением конкретных мер контроля. Следует напомнить, что в своей резолюции 1992/29 Экономический и Социальный Совет предложил "государствам, в которых изготавливаются прекурсоры и основные химические вещества, и государствам региона, в которых незаконно изготавливаются наркотические средства и психотропные вещества, установить тесное сотрудничество в целях предотвращения утечки прекурсоров и основных химических веществ в незаконные каналы". Совет далее настоятельно призвал страны, экспортирующие химические вещества, необходимые для незаконного производства героина и кокаина, обеспечить, чтобы компетентные органы при рассмотрении заявлений о предоставлении разрешений на экспорт "принимали разумные меры для проверки законного характера сделок в консультации, если это необходимо, со своими партнерами в импортирующих странах". Накопленный опыт свидетельствует о том, что установление в соответствующих случаях прямых контактов часто является средством наиболее оперативного выявления и пресечения подозрительных сделок в отношении веществ, находящихся под контролем.

Правительствам предлагается рассмотреть информацию по статье 12 Конвенции Организации Объединенных Наций о борьбе против незаконного оборота наркотических средств и психотропных веществ 1988 года и направить сообщения о любых изменениях по адресу: United Nations Office on Drugs and Crime, Secretariat of the International Narcotics Control Board, Vienna International Centre, P.O. Box 500, 1400 Vienna, Austria (факс: (+43-1) 26060-5867; адрес эл. почты: secretariat@incb.org).

1961 年《麻醉品单一公约》第 18 条和 1971 年《精神药物公约》第 16 条的 国家主管部门

本名录载列负责根据 1961 年《麻醉品单一公约》第 18 条和 1971 年《精神药物公约》第 16 条规定签发麻醉药品和精神药物进出口证书和准许证的所有国家主管部门。

这份国家部门名单是依照《1961 年公约》和《1971 年公约》印发的，沿用了 1931 年《限制和管制麻醉品运销公约》生效后的成规，《1946 年议定书》对该公约修订后将其纳入联合国的管理范围。本名录的内容根据国际药物管制条约缔约国和非缔约国在各相关的国际药物管制条约运作情况年度报告中向秘书长提供的数据编制而成。

本名录在第 18 条下列出的部门只负责签发麻醉药品的进出口准许证。

本名录在第 16 条下列出的部门只负责签发精神药物进出口准许证。

本名录在第 18 条和第 16 条下列出的部门既负责签发麻醉药品的也负责签发精神药物的进出口准许证。

本名录中部门名称前未列出这些公约条款号的，表示该国政府未指明该部门的职权范围。

如果本出版物在 1961 年《麻醉品单一公约》第 18 条和 1971 年《精神药物公约》第 16 条的国家主管部门下未列出一国或地区的联系地址，也有可能在 1988 年《联合国禁止非法贩运麻醉药品和精神药物公约》第 16 条的国家主管部门下列有可以使用的该国或该地区的联系地址。

请各国政府审查本名录所载资料，关于 1961 年《麻醉品单一公约》第 18 条和 1971 年《精神药物公约》第 16 条方面，如有改动，请通知联合国毒品和犯罪问题办公室，收件地址：United Nations Office on Drugs and Crime, Secretariat to the Governing Bodies, Vienna International Centre, P.O. Box 500, 1400 Vienna, Austria （传真号： +43-1-26060-5885； 电子邮箱： sgb@unodc.org）。

1988 年《联合国禁止非法贩运麻醉药品和精神药物公约》第 12 条的国家主管部门

本名录载列负责根据 1988 年《联合国禁止非法贩运麻醉药品和精神药物公约》第 12 条规定对前体和基本化学品实行监管或国家管制的所有国家主管部门。

这份国家部门名单是依照经济及社会理事会 1992 年 7 月 30 日第 1992/29 号决议印发的。其中内容根据各国政府向国际麻醉品管制局（麻管局）提供的数据编制。

秘书长曾向所有国家转递了普通照会，请各国提供负责执行《1988 年公约》第 12 条规定的国家主管部门的名称和地址。下列名单中没有星号的是各国政府在答复这些普通照会时所指明的国家部门。以星号(*)标出的是目前根据《1988 年公约》第 12 条第 12 款规定向麻管局提出报告但各国政府在答复普通照会时未加明确指明的国家主管部门。

如果本出版物在 1988 年《联合国禁止非法贩运麻醉药品和精神药物公约》第 12 条下未列出某一国家或地区的联系地址，也可能在 1961 年《麻醉品单一公约》第 18 条和 1971 年《精神药物公约》第 16 条的国家主管部门下列有可以使用的该国或该地区的联系地址。否则，可以联系麻管局秘书处或其他国际主管机构，查询进一步详情。这些国际机构的名称和地址列在本名录后。

必须了解负责执行具体管制措施的每个主管部门的各自职能和职责，才有可能在各国政府之间进行迅速而有效的信息交换。应当回顾，经济及社会理事会在其第 1992/29 号决议中，请"生产前体和基本化学品的国家及处于非法生产麻醉药品和精神药物的区域的国家建立密切合作关系，以防止前体和基本化学品转入非法渠道"。另外，经社理事会还促请海洛因和可卡因非法生产所需基本化学品的出口国确保主管部门在考虑出口准许证的申请时，"采取合理步骤，核实交易是否合法并酌情与进口国主管部门协商"。经验表明，酌情进行直接联系是发现和阻止涉及表列物品可疑交易的最迅捷手段。

请各国政府审查 1988 年《联合国禁止非法贩运麻醉药品和精神药物公约》第 12 条下的资料，如有改动，请通知联合国毒品和犯罪问题办公室，收件地址：United Nations Office on Drugs and Crime, Secretariat of the International Narcotics Control Board, Vienna International Centre, P.O. Box 500, 1400 Vienna, Austria（传真号：(+43-1) 26060-5867；电子邮箱：secretariat@incb.org）。

السلطات الوطنية المختصة بمقتضى المادة ١٨ من الاتفاقية الوحيدة للمخدرات لسنة ١٩٦١، والمادة ١٦ من اتفاقية المؤثرات العقلية لسنة ١٩٧١

ترد في هذا الدليل قائمة بجميع السلطات الوطنية المختصة المخوّلة إصدار الشهادات والأذون اللازمة لاستيراد وتصدير المخدرات والمؤثرات العقلية وفقا لأحكام المادة ١٨ من الاتفاقية الوحيدة للمخدرات لسنة ١٩٦١، والمادة ١٦ من اتفاقية المؤثرات العقلية لسنة ١٩٧١.

وتصدر هذه القائمة بالسلطات الوطنية عملا باتفاقيتي سنة ١٩٦١ وسنة ١٩٧١. وهي تتبع الممارسة التي استقرت بعد بدء نفاذ اتفاقية تحديد تصنيع المخدرات وتنظيم توزيعها لسنة ١٩٣١، التي وضعت تحت رعاية الأمم المتحدة بموجب بروتوكول سنة ١٩٤٦ المعدل لهذه الاتفاقية الأخيرة. وتستند محتويات القائمة إلى البيانات التي تقدمها إلى الأمين العام الدول الأطراف والدول غير الأطراف في المعاهدات الدولية لمراقبة المخدرات في تقاريرها عن سير هذه المعاهدات.

السلطات المشار إليها في هذا الدليل بمقتضى المادة ١٨ مخوّلة إصدار أذون استيراد وتصدير للمخدرات فقط.

والسلطات المشار إليها في هذا الدليل بمقتضى المادة ١٦ مخوّلة إصدار أذون استيراد وتصدير للمؤثرات العقلية فقط.

والسلطات المشار إليها في هذا الدليل بمقتضى المادتين ١٨ و١٦ مخوّلة إصدار أذون استيراد وتصدير للمخدرات والمؤثرات العقلية على السواء.

وعدم وجود إشارة إلى أي مادة من مواد هاتين الاتفاقيتين قبل اسم السلطة في هذا الدليل يعني أن الحكومة لم تحدد نطاق تخويل تلك السلطة المعنية.

وإذا لم يكن لبلد أو إقليم عنوان اتصال مدرج في هذا المنشور في إطار السلطات الوطنية المختصة بمقتضى المادة ١٨ من الاتفاقية الوحيدة للمخدرات لسنة ١٩٦١ والمادة ١٦ من اتفاقية المؤثرات العقلية لسنة ١٩٧١، فإن من المحتمل أن يكون لذلك البلد أو الإقليم عنوان اتصال مدرج يمكن استخدامه في إطار السلطات الوطنية المختصة بمقتضى المادة ١٢ من اتفاقية الأمم المتحدة لمكافحة الاتجار غير المشروع في المخدرات والمؤثرات العقلية لسنة ١٩٨٨.

ويرجى من الحكومات استعراض المعلومات الواردة في هذا الدليل وإبلاغ قسم دعم السياسات التابع لمكتب الأمم المتحدة المعني بالمخدرات والجريمة بأية تغييرات تطرأ فيما يتعلق بالمادة ١٨ من الاتفاقية الوحيدة للمخدرات لسنة ١٩٦١ والمادة ١٦ من اتفاقية المؤثرات العقلية لسنة ١٩٧١، على العنوان التالي: United Nations Office on Drugs and Crime, Secretariat to the Governing Bodies, Vienna International Centre, P.O. Box 500, 1400 Vienna, Austria (الفاكس: 26060-5885 (1-43+)؛ البريد الإلكتروني: sgb@unodc.org).

السلطات الوطنية المختصة بمقتضى المادة ١٢ من اتفاقية
الأمم المتحدة لمكافحة الاتجار غير المشروع في المخدرات
والمؤثرات العقلية لسنة ١٩٨٨

ترد في هذا الدليل أيضا قائمة بجميع السلطات الوطنية المختصة المخوّلة تنظيم أو إنفاذ الضوابط الرقابية الوطنية على السلائف والكيماويات الأساسية وفقا لأحكام المادة ١٢ من اتفاقية الأمم المتحدة لمكافحة الاتجار غير المشروع في المخدرات والمؤثرات العقلية لسنة ١٩٨٨.

وتصدر قائمة السلطات الوطنية عملا بقرار المجلس الاقتصادي والاجتماعي ٢٩/١٩٩٢ المؤرخ ٣٠ تموز/يوليه ١٩٩٢. وتستند محتويات القائمة إلى البيانات التي تقدّمها الحكومات إلى الهيئة الدولية لمراقبة المخدرات.

وقد أرسل الأمين العام مذكرات شفوية إلى جميع الدول طالبا أسماء وعناوين السلطات الوطنية المختصة المخوّلة تنفيذ أحكام المادة ١٢ من اتفاقية سنة ١٩٨٨. وترد تسميات السلطات الوطنية التي بيّنتها الحكومات ردّا على تلك المذكرات الشفوية في القائمة بدون علامة نجمية (٭). أما السلطات المؤشر عليها بعلامة نجمية، فهي السلطات الوطنية المختصة التي تقدم حاليا تقارير إلى الهيئة الدولية لمراقبة المخدرات بمقتضى أحكام الفقرة ١٢ من المادة ١٢ من اتفاقية سنة ١٩٨٨ ولكن الحكومات لم تحددها صراحة في ردودها على المذكرات الشفوية.

وإذا لم يكن لبلد أو إقليم عنوان اتصال مدرج في هذا المنشور في إطار السلطات الوطنية المختصة بمقتضى المادة ١٢ من اتفاقية الأمم المتحدة لمكافحة الاتجار غير المشروع في المخدرات والمؤثرات العقلية لسنة ١٩٨٨، فإن من المحتمل أن يكون لذلك البلد أو الإقليم عنوان اتصال يمكن استخدامه مدرج في إطار السلطات الوطنية المختصة بمقتضى المادة ١٨ من الاتفاقية الوحيدة للمخدرات لسنة ١٩٦١ وبمقتضى المادة ١٦ من اتفاقية المؤثرات العقلية لسنة ١٩٧١. وكخيار بديل يمكن الاتصال بأمانة الهيئة الدولية لمراقبة المخدرات أو غيرها من الهيئات الدولية المختصة للحصول على المزيد من المعلومات. وترد أسماء وعناوين تلك الهيئات الدولية في نهاية هذا الدليل.

ومن الضروري معرفة الأدوار والمسؤوليات المعهود بها إلى كل من السلطات المختصة فيما يتعلق بتنفيذ تدابير رقابية محددة حتى يتيسر تبادل المعلومات بين الحكومات بسرعة وفعالية. ويجدر التذكير بأن المجلس الاقتصادي والاجتماعي دعا في قراره ٢٩/١٩٩٢ "الدول التي تصنّع فيها السلائف والكيماويات الأساسية، ودول المنطقة التي تصنّع فيها المخدرات والمؤثرات العقلية على نحو غير مشروع، إلى أن تتعاون تعاونا وثيقا على منع تسريب السلائف والكيماويات الأساسية إلى القنوات غير المشروعة". وعلاوة على ذلك، حث المجلس الدول التي تصدّر كيماويات أساسية لإنتاج الهيروين والكوكايين على نحو غير مشروع على أن تضمن أن تقوم السلطات المختصة فيها، عند النظر في طلبات أذون التصدير، "باتخاذ تدابير معقولة للتحقق من مشروعية الصفقات، وعند الاقتضاء، بالتشاور في هذا الصدد مع السلطات المختصة في البلدان المستوردة". وقد تبيّن أن الاتصال المباشر، عند الاقتضاء، كثيرا ما يكون أسرع الوسائل لاستبانة ووقف الصفقات المشبوهة المشتملة على مواد مدرجة بالجداول.

ويرجى من الحكومات استعراض المعلومات فيما يتعلق بالمادة ١٢ من اتفاقية الأمم المتحدة لمكافحة الاتجار غير المشروع في المخدرات والمؤثرات العقلية لسنة ١٩٨٨ وإبلاغ مكتب الأمم المتحدة المعني بالمخدرات والجريمة بأية تغييرات تطرأ عليها، على العنوان التالي: United Nations Office on Drugs and Crime, Secretariat of the International Narcotics Control Board, Vienna International Centre, P.O. Box 500, 1400 Vienna, Austria (الفاكس: (1-43+) 26060-5867؛ البريد الإلكتروني: secretariat@incb.org.

Afghanistan — Afganistán

Articles 18, 16

Drug Regulation Committee
DRC/MCN, Banaye Bus Station, 9th District
Kabul
Afghanistan
Tel: 93 797 758 875
E-mail: nazari.razia@yahoo.com

Article 12

Director, Drug Regulation Committee Secretariat
Ministry of Counter Narcotics
Third Floor
Banayee Bus Station
Jalalabad Main Road
9th District
Kabul
Afghanistan
Tel: 93 7520 09959
Tel: 93 7005 25161
E-mail: drc_sec2007@yahoo.com

Albania — Albanie

Articles 18, 16, 12

Ministry of Health
Department of Pharmacy
Tirana
Albania
Tel: 355 42 364614
Fax: 355 42 364636
E-mail: ahysa@moh.gov.al

Algeria — Algérie — Argelia

Articles 18, 16

Direction Générale de la Pharmacie et des
    Equipements Médicaux
Ministère de la Santé, de la Population et de la
    Réforme Hospitalière.
125, boulevard Abderrahmane Laâla,
El Mouradia, Alger
Algérie
Tel: 2127 9628
Fax: 2127 9184

Article 12

Le Directeur de la pharmacie et du médicament
Ministère de la santé et de la population
125, rue Laala Abderrahmane
Alger
Algérie
Tel: 213 21 279 628
Fax: 213 21 279 184
Fax: 213 21 278 494
E-mail: msdphm@ibnsina.ands.dz

American Samoa - Samoa américain - Samoa Americana

See information immediately under United States of America, **Articles 18, 16**

Andorra — Andorre — Andorra

Articles 18, 16

Ministerio de Salut, Afers socials i Ocupació
Avda. Príncep Benlloch 30,
Edif. Clara Rabassa 4t
AD500 Andorra la Vella
500 Andorra
Tel: 376 865 465
Fax: 376 864 950
E-mail: interior_gov@andorra.ad

Article 12(*)

Servicio de Farmacia
Departamento de Recursos Sanitarios
Ministerio de Salud, Bienestar Social y Familia
Avda. Príncep Benlloch 26
Edificio Fundación Clara Rabassa
Andorra la Vella
Andorra
Tel: 376 874 800
Fax: 376 865 465
E-mail: ars@govern.ad

Angola

Articles 18, 16

National Directorate of Medicine
Rua Che-Guevara,
86, Maculusso/Ingombota
Luanda
Angola
Tel: 244 222 320 030
Fax: 244 222 328 166
E-mail: dnmedicamentos@ebonet

Anguilla — Anguila

Articles 18, 16

Director of Health Services
Ministry of Health
The Valley
Anguilla

Anguilla — Anguila
(continued — suite — continuación)

Article 12(*)

Attorney-General's Chambers
Government of Anguilla, The Secretariat
The Valley
Anguilla
Tel: 1 264 497 3185
Tel: 1 264 497 3044
Fax: 1 264 496 3126
E-mail: attorneygeneral@anguillanet.com

Antigua and Barbuda — Antigua-et-Barbuda — Antigua y Barbuda

Article 12

Chief Medical Officer, Medical Division
Ministry of Health and Home Affairs
Cross Street
St. John's
Antigua and Barbuda
Tel: 1 268 462 2675
Fax: 1 268 462 5003

Article 16

Chief Medical Officer, Medical Division
Ministry of Health and Home Affairs
Cross Street
St. John's
Antigua and Barbuda
Tel: 1 268 462 1600
Fax: 1 268 462 5003

Argentina — Argentine

Articles 18, 16

Dirección de Vigilancia de Sustancias Sujetas a Control
   Especial (INAME-ANMAT)
Adolfo Alsina 671 piso 4
Ciudad Autónoma de Buenos Aires
Tel: 54 11 4340 0800 (int. 5401)
Fax: 54 11 4340 0800 (int. 5408)
E-mail: nbelixan@anmat.gov.ar

Article 12

Director, Registro Nacional de Precursores Quimicos
   (RNPPRE)
Secretaria de Programacion para la Prevencion
   de la Drogadiccion y la Lucha contra el
   Narcotrafico de la Presidencia de la Nacion
   (SEDRONAR)
Sarmiento 624, Piso 3C1070AAP
Buenos Aires
Argentina
Tel: 54 11 4361 7810 extn.150
Fax: 54 11 4361 7810 111
E-mail: comercioexterior@renpre.gov.ar
E-mail: jdelosrios@sedronar.gov.arr

Overall coordination, certificates and licenses. Receives
pre-export notifications for Table I and II substances.

Article 12

Jefe, Departamento de Psicotrópicos y Estupefacientes
Ministerio de Salud y Acción Social
Administración Nacional de Medicamentos, Alimentos y
   Tecnología Médica (A.N.M.A.T.)
Av. Caseros 2161, 1er Piso
1264 Buenos Aires, C.F.
Argentina
Tel: 54 11 4340 0800
Tel: 54 11 4340 0900
Tel: 54 11 4340 0850
Fax: 54 11 4340 0853
E-mail: rmendez@anmat.gov.ar

Licit requirements for precursors.

Armenia — Arménie

Articles 18, 16

Ministry of Health of the Republic of Armenia
Government Republic Square Building 3
Yerevan 0010
Armenia
Tel: 374 10 582 413
Fax: 374 10 562 783
E-mail: info@moh.am
E-mail: minister@moh.am

Article 12

Police of the Republic of Armenia
Main Department on Combat Against Organized Crime
Department on Fight Against Illegal Drug Trafficking
Ministry of Interior
130 Nalbandian Street
Yerevan
Armenia
Tel: 374 10 587155
Fax: 374 10 587155
E-mail: antidrug@police.am
E-mail: ttdpv@mail.ru

Aruba

Articles 18, 16

Ministry of Health
Department of Medicine Inspection
Bernardstraat 75
San Nicolas
Aruba
Tel: 297 584 1199
Fax: 297 584 9143
E-mail: roselynn.angela@aruba.gov.aw

Article 12(*)

Director of Pharmaceutical Affairs
Bureau of Pharmaceutical Affairs
Bernhartstraat No. 75
San Nicolas
Aruba
Tel: 297 584 1199-302
Fax: 297 584 9143

Ascension Island – Île de l'Ascension – Isla de la Ascención

Article 12(*)

Senior Medical Officer,
Georgetown Hospital
Ascension Island
South Atlantic
Tel: 247 6010
Fax: 247 6011
E-mail: smo.hospital@ascension.gov.ac

Australia - Australie

Articles 18, 16

Drug Control Section
Office Scientific Evaluation
Therapeutic Goods Administration
Department of Health
Box 100
Woden ATC 2606
Australia
Tel: 61 2 6232 8740
Fax: 61 2 6203 1740
E-mail: dcs@tga.gov.au

Article 12

Director
Drug Control Section
Office of Scientific Evaluation
Therapeutic Goods Administration
Department of Health
PO Box 100, Woden ACT 2606
Australia
Tel: 61 2 6232 8740
Fax: 61 2 6203 1740
E-mail: dcs@tga.gov.au
Web: www.tga.gov.au

License and issue permits for importers, exporters of substances listed in Table I of the 1988 Convention. Control import/export of substances listed in Table II of the 1988 Convention. Receipt of pre-export notifications for substances listed in Table I and Table II of the 1988 Convention.

Austria - Autriche

Articles 18, 16

Federal Ministry of Health
Department II/A/5
Radetzkystrasse 2
1030 Vienna
Austria
Tel: 43 1 711 00 4787
Fax: 43 1 713 44 0416
E-mail: helmut.schroller@bmg.gv.at

Article 12

As regards legislation and coordination of administrative cooperation, please refer to entry of the European Union.

Federal Ministry of the Interior
Criminal Intelligence Service
Office 3.3.3
Precursor Control Unit
Josef Holaubek Platz 1
1090 Vienna
Austria
Tel: 43 1 24836 85351
Fax: 43 1 31925 63
E-mail: precursor@bmi.gv.at

Investigation in cases of diversion and other suspect activities; close contacts with the industry (manufacturers and traders) on a legal basis for the substances listed in Tables I and II and on a voluntary basis for substances not listed in the Tables.

Austria — Autriche
(continued — suite — continuación)

Article 12

As regards legislation and coordination of administrative cooperation, please refer to entry of the European Union.

Federal Ministry of Health
Department II/A/5
Radetzkystraße 2 A
1031 Vienna
Austria
Tel:　　43 1 711 00 4768
Fax:　　43 1 711 00 4652
E-mail:　wolfgang.pfneiszl@bmg.gv.at

General functions: Legal aspects; Coordination and cooperation with the other competent national authorities, the institutions of the European Union and the international bodies. Specific functions: Licensing and legislation of operators, issuing of export authorizations, monitoring of manufacture and domestic distribution.

Article 12

As regards legislation and coordination of administrative cooperation, please refer to entry of the European Union.

Federal Ministry of Finance
Department IV/3
Hintere Zollamtsstrasse 2B
1030 Vienna
Austria
Tel:　　43 1 51433 504086
Fax:　　43 1 51267 90
E-mail:　precursor@bmi.gv.at

Control/monitoring of exports, imports and transits at borders; investigation; prevention of fraud.

Azerbaijan - Azerbaïdjan - Azerbaiyán

Articles 18, 16

Republic Narcological Center
Zix Highway 13
Baku AZ1018
Azerbaijan
Tel:　　994 12 372 0607
Fax:　　994 12 372 9188
E-mail:　telman012@rambler.ru

Article 12

National Narcological Centre
Ministry of Health
Zykh Highway 13
Baku, AZ 1018
Azerbaijan
Tel:　　994 12 372 0607
Fax:　　994 12 372 9188
E-mail:　telman012@rambler.r

Bahamas

Articles 18, 16

National Drug Agency
Public Hospital Authority
P.O. Box N-8200
Nassau
Bahamas
Tel:　　1 242 328 6686
Fax:　　1 242 328 6665
E-mail:　bnda_bahamas@hotmail.com

Article 12

Comptroller of Customs
Ministry of Finance
P.O. Box N-155
Nassau
Bahamas
Tel:　　1 242 325 6551
Tel:　　1 242 326 4401/6
Fax:　　1 242 322 6223

Issues import/export authorizations.

Article 12

Chief Medical Officer
Ministry of Health
P.O. Box N-3730
Nassau
Bahamas
Tel:　　1 242 502 4853
Tel:　　1 242 502 4877
Tel:　　1 242 502 4727
Tel:　　1 242 502 4840
Fax:　　1 242 325 5421
E-mail:　mdr@batelnet.bs

Registration of chemical substances.

Bahrain — Bahreïn — Bahrein

Articles 18, 16

Pharmacy and Drug Control
Ministry of Health
P.O. Box 12
Manama
Bahrain
Tel:　　973 1 725 8668
Fax:　　973 1 725 9357

Article 12(*)

Director, Criminal Investigation Directorate
Ministry of Interior
P.O. Box 13
Manama
Bahrain
Tel: 973 1 718 888
Fax: 973 1 270 463
Fax: 973 1 714 760

Bangladesh

Articles 18, 16

Department of Narcotics Control (DNC)
Ministry of Home Affairs
Wage Earners Hostel Complex (Level-8)
71-72, Old Elephant Road (Eskaton Garden),
    Ramna
Dhaka 1000
Bangladesh
Tel: 880 2 831 2131
Fax: 880 2 831 1155
E-mail: dgdnc@bttb.net.bd

Article 12

Director-General, Department of Narcotics
    Control
Ministry of Home Affairs
441, Tejgaon Industrial Area
Dhaka 1208
Bangladesh
Tel: 880 2 8870 011
Fax: 880 2 8870 010
E-mail: dgdncbd@gmail.com
Web: www.dnc.gov.bd

Import, export, transport, possession, use, sale,
purchase, warehousing, processing, etc.

Barbados — Barbade

Articles 18, 16

Director, Barbados Drug Service
Ministry of Health
Jemott's Lane, St. Michael
Bridgetown
Barbados
Tel: 1 246 426 5080/Ext. 226
Tel: 1 246 427 8309
Tel: 1 246 426 5080/Ext. 224
Fax: 1 246 429 6980

Article 12(*)

Director, Barbados Drug Service
Ministry of Health
Jemott's Lane, St. Michael
Bridgetown
Barbados
Tel: 1 246 426 5080/Ext. 224-226
Tel: 1 246 427 8309
Fax: 1 246 429 6980

Belarus — Bélarus — Belarús

Articles 18, 16

Head of Department of Pharmaceutical
    Inspections and Medicine Provision
Ministry of Health
Miasnikova str. 39
220048 Minsk
Belarus
Tel: 375 17 222 7081
Tel: 375 17 200 7104
Fax: 375 17 222 6297
Fax: 375 17 200 6390
E-mail: lreutskaya@belcmt.by
E-mail: gpyshnik@belcmt.by

Articles 18, 16

Department of Drugs and Human Trafficking
    Prevention
Ministry of the Interior
Gorodskoy Val street 2
220050 Minsk
Belarus
Tel: 375 17 218 7521
E-mail: dnk_mvd@mail.ru

Article 12

Ministry of Health
39, Miasnikova str.
220048 Minsk
Belarus
Tel: 375 17 222 6547
Fax: 375 17 2226 297

Belgium — Belgique — Bélgica

Articles 18, 16

L'Agence féderale des médicaments et produits
    de santé (Afmps)
Service des Stupéfiants
Place Victor Horta 40/40, Eurostation II
1060 Bruxelles
Tel: 32 2 524 8265
Fax: 32 2 524 8383
E-mail: narcotics@fagg-afmps.be

Belgium — Belgique — Bélgica
(continued — suite — continuación)

Article 12

As regards legislation and coordination of administrative cooperation, please refer to entry of the European Union.

Federal Agency for Medicines and Health Products
Drug Precursors Unit
Eurostation Bloc II - 8th Floor
Place Victor Horta, 40,box 40
1060 Bruxelles
Belgium
Tel: 32 2 524 8311/12
Fax: 32 2 524 8319
E-mail: drugprecursor@fagg-afmps.be

Authorization of commerce and exportation. Legislation and administrative cooperation.

Article 12

As regards legislation and coordination of administrative cooperation, please refer to entry of the European Union.

Federal Police
Central Office Drugs, Office Synthetic Drugs
Rue Fritz Toussaint 47
1050 Brussels
Belgium
Tel: 32 2 642 7894
Fax: 32 2 642 6955
E-mail: dgj.djp.drugs.ops@police.be

Control and investigation.

Article 12

As regards legislation and coordination of administrative cooperation, please refer to entry of the European Union.

Interpol Belgique
Rue des Quatre Bras 13
1000 Bruxelles
Belgique
Tel: 32 2 508 7372
Fax: 32 2 511 9249

Investigation.

Article 12

As regards legislation and coordination of administrative cooperation, please refer to entry of the European Union.

Customs and Excises
Drug Precursor Unit
North Galaxy Tour A/9
Boulevard du Roi Albert II, 33/385
1030 Brussels, Belgium
Tel: 322 57 65560
Fax: 322 57 96613
E-mail: da.oo.precursors@minfin.fed.beminfin.fed.be

Belize — Belice

Articles 18, 16

Ministry of Health
3rd floor, East Block Building
Belmopan City
Belize
Tel: 501 822 0809
Fax: 501 822 2942
E-mail: dhs@health.gov.bz

Benin — Bénin

Articles 18, 16

Comité Interministériel de lutte contre la drogue
B.P. 353
Cotonou
Bénin
Tel: 229 21 31 12 33
Fax: 229 21 31 12 33

Article 12

Brigade des moeurs et stupéfiants
B.P. 353
Cotonou
Bénin
Tel: 229 21 31 38 0

Fight against illicit abuse and trafficking.

Article 12

Directeur des pharmacies et des explorations
   diagnostiques
Ministère de la santé publique
B.P. 2048
Cotonou
Bénin
Tel: 229 21 30 02 47
Fax: 229 21 30 74 80

Controls and issues licenses of imports and exports.

Bermuda - Bermudes - Bermudas

Articles 18, 16

The Chief Medical Officer, Department of Health
Ministry of Health and Social Services
P.O. Box HM 1195
Hamilton HM EX
Bermuda
Tel: 1 441 236 4902
Fax: 1 441 236 1215

Article 12(*)

The Chief Medical Officer, Department of Health
Ministry of Health and Social Services
P.O. Box HM 1195
Hamilton HM EX
Bermuda
Tel: 1 441 278 4900
Fax: 1 441 292 2629

Bhutan — Bhoutan — Bhután

Articles 18, 16

Director, Department of Revenues and Customs
Ministry of Finance
Thimphu
Bhutan
Tel: 975 2 23057
Fax: 975 2 22306

Article 12(*)

Director General
Bhutan Narcotic Control Agency (BNCA)
Post Box 429
Thimphu
Bhutan
Tel: 975 2 335 371
Fax: 975 2 335 370
E-mail: plwangdi@hotmail.com
E-mail: bnca_pharm@yahoo.com

Responsible for registration, issuing of import/export authorizations, investigation and licensing.

Bolivia (Plurinational State of) — Bolivie (État plurinational de) — Bolivia (Estado Plurinacional de)

Articles 18, 16

Unidad de Medicamentos y Tecnología en Salud
(UNIMED)
Ministerio de Salud y Deportes
Calle Capitán Ravelo No. 2199
La Paz
Estado Plurinacional de Bolivia
Tel: 591 2 244 4432
Fax: 591 2 244 0122
E-mail: delia_villarroel@hotmail.com

Article 12

Directora, Dirección de Medicamentos y
Tecnología en Salud
Ministerio de Salud y Deportes
Calle Capitán Ravelo No. 2199
La Paz
Estado Plurinacional de Bolivia
Tel: 591 2 244 0122
Fax: 591 2 244 0122

Control of ephedrine, pseudoephedrine, ergometrine and ergotamine.

Article 12

Dirección General de Sustancias Controladas
(DGSC)
Vice Ministerio de Defensa Social y Sustancias
Controladas
Ministerio de Gobierno
Av. Arce n°2142 entre Fernando Guachalla y
Aspiazu, frente al Ministerio de Educación
La Paz
Plurinational State of Bolivia
Tel: 591 2 214 5514
Tel: 591 2 211 7037
Tel: 591 2 214 5516
Fax: 591 2 214 5514 302
Fax: 591 2 214 5516 205
Fax: 591 2 214 5516 302
Fax: 591 2 211 7037 205
Fax: 591 2 214 5514 205
Fax: 591 2 241 6290
Fax: 591 2 211 7037 302
E-mail: sistemas@dgsc.gob.bo
E-mail: notificaciones@dgsc.gob.bo

Bosnia and Herzegovina — Bosnie-Herzégovine — Bosnia y Herzegovina

Articles 18, 16

Ministry of Security of Bosnia and Herzegovina
Trg BiH 3
Bosnia and Herzegovina
Tel: 387 33 492 708
Fax: 387 3321 6024
E-mail: lejla.copelj@msb.gov.ba

Articles 18, 16

Agency for Medicines and Medical Products
Ulica Veljka Mladenovica bb
78000 Banja Luka
Bosnia and Herzegovina
Tel: 387 51 456 040
Tel: 387 51 456 050
Fax: 387 51 450 301

Bosnia and Herzegovina — Bosnie-Herzégovine — Bosnia y Herzegovina
(continued — suite — continuación)

Article 12

Assistant to the Minister
Federal Ministry of Internal Affairs
71000 Sarajevo
Bosnia and Herzegovina
Tel: 387 33 280 020 - 3320
Fax: 387 33 590 218
E-mail: dompolicije@@bih.net.ba
E-mail: medjunarodna@fmup.gov.ba

Article 12

Director, Agency for Medicines and Medical Products
Ulica Veljka Mladenovica bb
78000 Banja Luka
Bosnia and Herzegovina
Tel: 387 51 456 040
Tel: 387 51 456 050
Tel: 387 51 420 302
Fax: 387 51 450 266
Fax: 387 51 450 301
E-mail: klinicka@alims.gov.ba
E-mail: tijana.s@alims.gov.ba

Issue export and import authorizations of narcotic drugs and their preparations listed in Schedules I, II, III and IV of the 1961 Convention, psychotropic substances listed in Schedules I, II, III and IV of the 1971 Convention and substances listed in Tables I and II of the 1988 Convention.

Botswana

Articles 18, 16

Ministry of Health
Private Bag 0038
Gaborone
Botswana
Tel: 267 395 2264
Fax: 267 317 0169
E-mail: jbotsang@gov.bw

Article 12

Principal Pharmacist 1, Drugs Regulatory Unit
Ministry of Health
Floor 7, Poso House, Khama Crescent,
Private Bag 0038
Gaborone
Botswana
Tel: 267 363 2376
Fax: 267 317 0169
Fax: 267 317 0172
E-mail: dunit@gov.bw

Control of imports, exports, manufacture and distribution of drugs and related substances.

Article 12(*)

Chief Pharmacist, Drugs Regulatory Unit
Ministry of Health Headquarters
Government Enclave
3rd Floor, Block D
Gaborone
Botswana
Tel: 267 363 2064
Tel: 267 363 2378
Fax: 267 317 0172
Fax: 267 317 0169
E-mail: dunit@gov.bw

Brazil — Brésil — Brasil

Articles 18, 16

National Health Surveillance Agency (ANVISA)
SIA Trecho 5, Área Especial 57, Bloco D
CEP 71.205-050 Brasilia, D.F.
Brazil
Tel: 55 61 3462 5429
Fax: 55 61 3462 5833
E-mail: med.controlados@anvisa.gov.br
E-mail: rel@anvisa.gov.br

Article 12

Jefe, Division de Control de Productos Quimicos-
   DCPQ/CGPRE/DCOR
Departamento de Policia Federal
Ministerio de Justicia
EQSW 103/104, Quadra 1, Bloco A
Setor Sudoeste
CEP:70.670-350 Brasilia, D.F.
Brazil
Tel: 55 61 2024 9600
Fax: 55 61 3311 9630
E-mail: ccpq.cgpre@dpf.gov.br

Article 12(*)

Chemicals products control.
Director-Presidente, Agencia Nacional de
   Vigilancia Sanitaria (ANVISA)
SIA, Trecho 5, Área Especial 57
CEP 71205-050 Brasilia, D.F.
Brasil
Tel: 55 61 3462 5402
Tel: 55 61 3462 5406
Fax: 55 61 3462 5321
E-mail: med.controlados@anvisa.gov.br

Controls imports and exports of substances included in Table I of 1988 Convention; receives pre-export notifications for Table I substances and for anthranilic acid, phenylacetic acid and piperidine.

British Virgin Islands —
Îles Vierges britanniques —
Islas Vírgenes Británicas

Articles 18, 16

Ministry of Health, Education and Welfare
Road Town
Tortola
British Virgin Islands
Tel: 1 284 494 3701

Article 12

Director of Health Services
Ministry of Health and Social Development
Central Administration Complex
33 Admin Drive,Road Town
Tortola VG1110
British Virgin Islands
Tel: 1 284 494 3701 Ext. 2174
Fax: 1 284 494 5018
E-mail: ministryofhealth@gov.vg
E-mail: grwheatley@go.vg

Monitoring the importation/exportation and use of narcotics and psychotropic substances.

Brunei Darussalam —
Brunéi Darussalam

Article 18

Minister for Health
Ministry of Health
Jalan Menteri Besar
Bandar Seri Begawan BB3910
Brunei Darussalam
Tel: 673 2 381 640
Fax: 673 2 381 980

Article 16

Poisons Licensing Officer
Ministry of Health
Jalan Menteri Besar
Bandar Seri Begawan BB3910
Brunei Darussalam
Tel: 673 2 381 640
Fax: 673 2 380 687

Article 12

Narcotics Control Bureau
Prime Minister's Office
Jalan Tungku, Gadong
Bandar Seri Begawan BE 2110
Brunei Darussalam
Tel: 673 2448 877
Fax: 673 2422 477
E-mail: muinuddin.rahman@narcotics.gov.bn
E-mail: liaison@narcotics.gov.bn

Law enforcement; investigations of diversion and controlled deliveries.

Article 12

Royal Customs and Excise Department
Ministry of Finance
Bandar Seri Begawan 2045
Brunei Darussalam
Tel: 673 2 422 480
Tel: 673 2 448 877
Tel: 673 2 422 479
Tel: 673 2 243 342
Fax: 673 2 422 464
Fax: 673 2 242 600
E-mail: ncb@brunet.bn

Suppression of illicit traffic.

Article 12

Director, Department of Pharmaceutical Services
Ministry of Health
Simpang 433, Kg. Madaras, Jalan Utama Terunjing
Mukim Gadong
Brunei Darussalam
Tel: 673 2393 298
Fax: 673 2393 096
E-mail: pharmacy.services@moh.gov.bn

Responsible for the illicit import and use of precursors.

Bulgaria — Bulgarie

Articles 18, 16

Ministry of Health, "Medical Products, medical devices
    and narcotic drugs"
Directorate "Narcotic Drugs" Department
5, Sveta Nedelja Sq.
1000 Sofia
Bulgaria
Tel: 359 2 9301 220
Fax: 359 2 9301 220
E-mail: fmihaylova@mh.government.bg

Bulgaria — Bulgarie
(continued — suite — continuación)

Article 12

As regards legislation and coordination of administrative cooperation, please refer to entry of the European Union.

Director, National Service "Counter Organized
  Crime" (NSCOC)
Ministry of Interior
127A, Cherni Vruh Blvd
1407 Sofia
Bulgaria
Tel: 359 2 988 5288
Fax: 359 2 988 5922
Fax: 359 2 988 5902

Responsible for fight against diversion of chemical substances. Executes controlled deliveries. Responsibility for seizures, law enforcement and investigation.

Article 12

As regards legislation and coordination of administrative cooperation, please refer to entry of the European Union.

Head, Drug Enforcement Division
General Customs Directorate
Ministry of Finance
1, Aksakov Str.
1040 Sofia
Bulgaria
Tel: 359 2 869 562
Fax: 359 2 980 3251

Coordinates customs monitoring of import, export and transit.

Article 12

As regards legislation and coordination of administrative cooperation, please refer to entry of the European Union.

The Joint Committee for Control of Precursors (JCCP)
Ministry of Economy, Energy and Tourism
8, Slavianska Street
1052 Sofia
Bulgaria
Tel: 359 2 940 7873
Fax: 359 2 980 4710
E-mail: skoleva@mee.government.bg

Licenses the manufacturers, importers and exporters of the substances listed in Tables I and II of the 1988 Convention and issues import and export permits.

Burkina Faso

Articles 18, 16

Direction générale de la pharmacie, du médicament et
  des laboratoires (DGPML)/Ministre de la Santé
03 B.P. 7009
Ouagadougou 03
Burkina Faso
Tel: 226 50 3246 60
E-mail: jbnikiema@yahoo.fr

Article 12

Le Ministre de la santé publique
Ministère de la santé
03 BP 7035
Ouagadougou 03
Burkina Faso
Tel: 226 50 326 188
Fax: 226 50 317 024

Issues import/export authorization.

Article 12

Comité National de Lutte contre la Drogue
Ministère de la sécurité
B.P. 5175
Ouagadougou 01
Burkina Faso
Tel: 226 50 316 812
Tel: 226 50 316 595
Fax: 226 50 315 887

Law enforcement.

Burundi

Articles 18, 16

Director, Department of Pharmacies, Medicines and
  Laboratories
B.P. 1820
Bujumbura
Burundi
Tel: 257 7942 3466
Tel: 257 2227 3255
E-mail: mpaweser2000@yahoo.fr

Cabo Verde

Articles 18, 16

Direction générale des pharmacies
Ministère de la santé
B.P. 47
Praia - Santiago
Cape Verde
Tel: 238 261 0112
Fax: 238 261 3585
E-mail: edith.santos@ms.gov.cv

Article 12

Directeur Général des pharmacies
Ministère de la santé
B.P. 47
Praia - Santiago
Cape Verde
Tel: 238 261 0112
Fax: 238 261 0163
Fax: 238 261 3991
E-mail: edith.santos@ms.gov.cv

Implementing article 12 of the 1988 Convention.

Cambodia — Cambodge — Camboya

Article 12(*)

Camcontrol
Ministry of Commerce
Phnom Penh
Cambodia

Article 12(*)

Chief, Narcotic Control and Pharmaceutical Trade
  Bureau
Department of Drugs and Food
Ministry of Health
No. 8 Street Ong Pokoun, No. 153/154 Kampuchea
Krom Road
Phnom Penh
Cambodia
Tel: 855 12 959 726
Tel: 855 12 824 874
Fax: 855 23 880 247
Fax: 855 23 884 330
E-mail: moh-cpn@forum.org.kh

(Article not specified)

State Secretary for Public Health
Phnom Penh
Cambodia

Cameroon — Cameroun — Camerún

Articles 18, 16

Ministère de la Santé Publique
Direction de la Pharmacie et du Médicament
Yaoundé
Cameroun
Tel: 237 22 22 41 44
Fax: 237 22 23 39 33

Article 12

Ministère de la Santé Publique
Direction de la Pharmacie et du Médicament
Yaoundé
Cameroun
Tel: 237 22 22 41 44
Fax: 237 22 23 39 33

Article 12

Ministère de la Santé Publique
Direction de la Promotion de la Santé
Comité National de Lutte contre la Drogue (CNLD)
Yaoundé
Cameroun
Tel: 237 22 23 12 84
Fax: 237 22 23 12 85

Canada - Canadá

Articles 18, 16

Health Canada
150 Tunney's Pasture Driveway
Tunney's Pasture
Room 1605-618
Ottawa, Ontario K1A 0K9
Canada
Tel: 1 613 941 1977
Fax: 1 613 946 6460
E-mail: suzy.mcdonald@hc-sc.gc.ca

Article 12

Director General
Office of Controlled Substances
Controlled Substances and Tobacco Directorate
Healthy Environments and Consumer Safety Branch
Health Canada
150 Tunney's Pasture Driveway
A.L. 0301 A
Ottawa, Ontario K1A 0K9
Canada
Tel: 1 613 952 2177
Fax: 1 613 946 4224
E-mail: jacqueline.goncalves@hc-sc.gc.ca c.ca

Canada — Canadá
(continued — suite — continuación)

Article 12

Director, International Crime and Terrorism
  Division (IDT)
Foreign Affairs, Trade and Development Canada
Lester B. Pearson Building
125 Sussex Drive
Ottawa, Ontario K1A OG2
Canada
Tel: 1 613 996 1430
Fax: 1 613 944 4827

Export control.

Cayman Islands – Îles Caïmanes – Islas Caimanes

Articles 18, 16

Chief Medical Officer
The Pharmacy Board
P.O. Box 915 GT
Grand Cayman
Cayman Islands KYI-1103
Tel: 1 345 949 8604

Article 12

Chief Medical Officer, Health Services
  Department
P.O. Box 915, George Town
Grand Cayman
Cayman Islands, KYI-1103
West Indies
Tel: 1 345 949 8600
Fax: 1 345 244 2714
E-mail: Delroy.Jefferson@hsa.ky

Central African Republic — République centrafricaine — República Centroafricana

Article 18

Ministère de la santé publique et de la population
Bangui
République centrafricaine
Tel: 236 21 612 901

Article 16

Directeur des médicaments
Ministère de la santé publique et de la population
Bangui
République centrafricaine
Tel: 236 21 611 520

Article 12

L'Inspecteur des services pharmaceutiques
Inspection centrale des services pharmaceutiques
Ministère de la santé publique et de la population
B.P. 883
Bangui
République centrafricaine
Tel: 236 506 528 (Home)
Tel: 236 613 188 (Bureau)
Fax: 236 611 175
E-mail: mspp@intnet.cf

Control of imports, exports, manufacture and distribution of pharmaceutical products.

Article 12

Direction de l'office central de lutte antidrogue
B.P. 790
Bangui
République centrafricaine
Tel: 236 617 166
Fax: 236 617 532

Law enforcement.

Chad – Tchad

Articles 18, 16

Bureau des stupéfiants
Inspection des pharmacies
Division pharmacies/DES/MSP
B.P. 1948
N'Djamena
Tchad
Tel: 235 518 966
Tel: 235 515 587
Fax: 235 515 587
Fax: 235 519 035

Article 12(*)

Directeur, Direction de la pharmacie, du médicament et
　des laboratoires
Service Inspection
Bureau des stupéfiants
Ministère de la santé publique
B.P. 1948
N'Djamena
Tchad
Tel:　　235 22 515 587
Fax:　　235 22 517 408
E-mail:　divpharm@intnet.td
E-mail:　cpa.tschad@intnet.td

Chile — Chili

Articles 18, 16

Área Sustancias Quimicas Controladas, Ministerio del
　Interior y Seguridad Pública
Palacio de la Moneda S/N
Santiago
Chile
Tel:　　56 2 2694 5640
E-mail:　sperello@interior.gov.cl

Article 12

Directora, Instituto de Salud Pública
Ministerio de Salud
Avda. Marathon 1000 Ñuñoa-Casilla 48
Santiago
Chile
Tel:　　56 2 575 5106
Tel:　　56 2 575 5100
Fax:　　56 2 575 5658
Fax:　　56 2 575 5662

Issues authorizations for the use of precursors used in
the manufacture of pharmaceutical products.

Article 12

Jefe
Departamento de Sustancias Químicas Controladas,
　de la División de Estudios de la Subsecretaría
　del Interior
Ministerio del Interior
Edificio Moneda Bicentenario
Teatino 92
Santiago, Chile
Tel:　　56 2 2694 5640
E-mail:　quimicos@interior.gov.cl
E-mail:　sperello@interior.cl

Coordinating agency for the implementation of article 12
of the 1988 Convention.

China — Chine

Articles 18, 16

China Food and Drug Administration
26 Xuanwumen Xidajie
100053 Beijing
China
Tel:　　86 10 8833 0838
Fax:　　86 10 6833 6683
E-mail:　liwh@cfda.gov.cn

Article 12

Secretary-General
Office of the National Narcotics Control Commission
14 Dong Chang An Street
100741 Beijing
China
Tel:　　86 10 6626 2595
Tel:　　86 10 6626 2718
Fax:　　86 10 5818 6577
E-mail:　shanxiaojing@sohu.com
E-mail:　13911253536@163.com
E-mail:　wenzr@139.com

Article 12(*)

China Food and Drug Administration
26 Xuanwumen Xidajie
100053 Beijing
China
Tel:　　86 10 8833 0838
Fax:　　86 10 6833 6683
E-mail:　liwh@cfda.gov.cn

Christmas Island –
Île Christmas –
Isla Christmas

Articles 18, 16

Drug Control Section, Office of Scientific Evaluation
Therapeutic Goods Administration
Department of Health
P.O. Box 100
Woden ACT 2606
Australia
Tel:　　61 2 6232 8740
Fax:　　61 2 6203 1740
E-mail:　dcs@tga.gov.au

Christmas Island –
Île Christmas –
Isla Christmas
(continued — suite — continuación)

Article 12

Director
Drug Control Section, Office of Scientific Evaluation
Therapeutic Goods Administration
Department of Health
PO Box 100
Woden ACT 2606, Australia
Tel: 61 2 6232 8740
Fax: 61 26203 1740
E-mail: dcs@tga.gov.au
Web: www.tga.gov.au

Cocos (Keeling) Islands –
Îles des Cocos (Keeling) –
Islas Cocos (Keeling)

Articles 18, 16

Drug Control Section, Office of Scientific Evaluation
Therapeutic Goods Administration
Department of Health
P.O. Box 100
Woden ACT 2606
Australia
Tel: 61 2 6232 8740
Fax: 61 2 6203 1740
E-mail: dcs@tga.gov.au

Article 12

Director
Drug Control Section, Office of Scientific Evaluation
Therapeutic Goods Administration
Department of Health
PO Box 100
Woden ACT 2606,
Australia
Tel: 61 2 6232 8740
Fax: 61 2 6203 1740
E-mail: dcs@tga.gov.au
Web: www.tga.gov.au

Colombia — Colombie

Articles 18, 16, 12

U.A.E Fondo Nacional de Estupefacientes
Av. Caracas No. 1-85 Sur
Bogotá
Colombia
Tel: 57 1 333 1088
Fax: 57 1 280 1263
E-mail: direccion@fne.gov.co
E-mail: coordinacionivc@fne.gov.co

Article 12

Dirección de Política Contra las Drogas y Actividades
    Relacionadas
Subdirección de Control y Fiscalización de Sustancias
    Químicas y Estupefacientes
Ministerio de Justicia y del Derecho
Calle 53 No. 13-27
Bogota
Colombia
Tel: 571 444 31 00 Ext. 1267
Fax: 571 444 31 00 Ext. 1223
E-mail: controlyfiscalizacionsustanciasn@minjusticia.gov.co
E-mail: consultas.tramitessq@minjusticia.gov.coo

Import and export authorizations for Table II substances;
receives pre-export notifications for Table II substances.

Article 12

Dirección de Impuestos y Aduanas Nacionales DIAN
Carrera 8 Nº 6C - 38 Edificio San Agustín
Bogotá – Colombia
Tel: 57 1 607 9999
Fax: 57 1 607 9416
E-mail: mguzmanr@dian.gov.co.
E-mail: ncastiblancoa3@dian.gov.co

Article 12

Dirección Antinarcóticos
Policía Nacional de Colombia
Aeropuerto Internacional el Dorado - Entrada No. 6,
Dirección de Antinarcóticos
Bogotá – Colombia
Tel: 57 1 439 7436
Tel: 57 1 439 7435
Fax: 57 1 315 9271
E-mail: diran.jefat@policia.gov.co

Law enforcement/Criminal offences.

Article 12

Directora
Unidad Administrativa Especial
Fondo Nacional de Estupefacientes
Ministerio de la Salud y Protección Social
Avenida Caracas No.1-85 Sur Bogotá
Colombia
Tel: 57 1 333 1088
Fax: 57 1 280 1263
E-mail: direccion@fne.gov.co

Comoros — Comores — Comoras

(Article not specified)

Inspection des pharmacies
Département des services de la santé
Moroni
Comores

Congo

Articles 18, 16

Direction des pharmacies et des laboratoires
B.P. 78
Brazzaville
Congo
Tel: 242 28 832 298

Article 12

Chercheur chimiste
Ministère de la science et de la technologie
B.P. 1249 Cerve
Brazzaville
Congo
Tel: 242 28 664 8479
E-mail: droguedgrst@yahoo.fr

Cook Islands – Îles Cook – Islas Cook

Articles 18, 16

Secretary, Ministry of Health
P.O. Box 109
Rarotonga
Cook Islands
Tel: 682 29664
Fax: 682 23109
E-mail: soh1@health.gov.ck

Article 12

Ministry of Finance and Economic Management Revenue
Management Division, Customs
Revenue Management Division, Customs
P.O. Box 99, Avarua
Rarotonga
Cook Islands
Tel: 682 29365
Fax: 682 29465

Law enforcement and investigation.

Article 12(*)

Secretary, Ministry of Health
P.O. Box 109
Rarotonga
Cook Islands
Tel: 682 29664 ext.712/713
Fax: 682 23109
E-mail: aremaki@health.gov.ck

Overall coordination.

Costa Rica

Articles 18, 16

Junta de Vigilancia de Drogas Estupefacientes
Ministerio de Salud
Apdo. 10123-1000
San José
Costa Rica
Tel: 506 2223 0333 ext. 224
Fax: 506 2257 7827
E-mail: fsaborio@ministeriodesalud.go.cr

Article 12

Jefe, Unidad de Control y Fiscalización de Precursores
Instituto Costarricense Sobre Drogas
Ministerio de la Presidencia
Apartado 7311-1000
San José
Costa Rica
Tel: 506 2527 6433
Tel: 506 2527 6439
Tel: 506 2527 6435
Tel: 506 2527 6434
Fax: 506 2524 0234
E-mail: precucr@icd.go.cr
E-mail: eramirez@icd.go.cr

Costa Rica
(continued — suite — continuación)

Article 12

Policía de Control de Drogas
Ministerio de Seguridad Pública
Desamparados, de la rotonda de Desamparado
San José
Costa Rica
Tel: 506 2227 6352
Fax: 506 2227 8910
E-mail: asolano@seguridadpublica.go.cr

Research irregular shifts the UNFP cases (Unidad de Control y Fiscalización de Precursores), investigation of cases involving precursors that can result from drug-related research, care alerts. International police forces, which are related to precursors.

Article 12

Unidad de Asesoría Legal del Instituto Costarricense Sobre
Drogas
San Pedro de Montes de Oca
Barrio Dent, de la Agencia Hyundai 375 m norte, contiguo al Restaurante Jurgen's
San José
Costa Rica
Tel: 506 2527 6441
Fax: 506 2524 0148
E-mail: jastua@icd.go.cr

Article 12

Fiscalía Adjunta Contra la Delincuencia Organizada
Ministerio Público
Barrio González Lahmann
Edificios de la Corte Suprema de Justicia
San José
Costa Rica
Tel: 506 2295-3873
Fax: 506 2223 6034
E-mail: wespinoza@Poder-Judicial.go.cr

Côte d'Ivoire

Articles 18, 16

Direction de la pharmacie et du médicament
B.P. V5
Abidjan
Côte d'Ivoire
Tel: 225 21 351 323
Tel: 225 21 357 313
Fax: 225 21 356 958
E-mail: info@dpmci.org

Article 12

Directeur, Direction de la pharmacie et du médicament
Ministère de la santé publique
52 Boulevard de Marseille, B.P. 5
Abidjan
Côte d'Ivoire
Tel: 225 21 357 313
Fax: 225 21 356 958
E-mail: rachdunc2002@yahoo.fr

Control of imports, stocks and distribution.

Article 12

Direction de la Police des stupéfiants et des drogues
Service de répression
Ministère de la sécurité
B.P.2382
Abidjan 8
Côte d'Ivoire
Tel: 225 20 224 838
Tel: 225 20 224 807
Fax: 225 20 215 314
E-mail: abdoubinate@hotmail.com

Suppression of drug abuse.

Article 12

Direction Générale des Douanes
Subdivision des stupéfiants
BP V25 Abidjan
Côte d'Ivoire
Tel: 225 2031 2766
E-mail: glgiap@yahoo.fr

Croatia — Croatie — Croacia

Articles 18, 16

Ministry of Health and Social Welfare
Ksaver 200A
10000 Zagreb
Croatia
Tel: 385 1 460 7541
Fax: 385 1 460 7755

Article 12

Head, Department for Drugs
Ministry of Health and Welfare
Ksaver 200a
10000 Zagreb
Croatia
Tel: 385 1 460 7541
Fax: 385 1 467 7105

Croatia — Croatie — Croacia
(continued — suite — continuación)

Article 12

Head, Office for Combating Narcotic Drugs Abuse
Preobraženska 4/II
10000 Zagreb
Croatia
Tel: 385 1 487 8128
Fax: 385 1 487 8120
E-mail: ured@uredzadroge.hr
Web: http:/www.uredzadroge.hr

Article 12

Minister for Health and Social Welfare
Ministry of Health and Social Welfare
Ksaver 200a
10000 Zagreb
Croatia
Tel: 385 1 467 7089
Fax: 385 1 467 7091

Cuba

Articles 18, 16

Ministerio de Salud Pública
Calle 23, No. 177, entre las calles M y N
Vedado, Plaza de la Revolución
Zona Postal Habana 4
Ciudad de La Habana
Cuba
Tel: 53 7 202 9969
E-mail: desp@infomed.sld.cu

Article 12

Director
Sección de Control de Estupefacientes,
   Sicotropicos y Similares
Departamento de Atención a los Servicios
   Farmacéuticos
Área de Asistencia Médica y Social
Dirección Nacional de Medicamentos y Tecnologias
Ministerio de Salud Pública
Calle 23 No. 201, Piso 7, e/M y N, Vedado
Municipio Plaza de la Revolución
La Habana
Cuba
Tel: 53 7 838 3395
Tel: 53 7 838 3393
Tel: 53 7 831 9366
Fax: 53 7 833 2312
E-mail: dnatencionmedica@infomed.sld.cu
E-mail: desp@infomed.sld.cu
E-mail: dfo@infomed.sld.cu

General functions: Controls import, export, manufacture, storage and use of substances included in Tables I and II of the 1988 Convention. Specific functions: Proposes and elaborates control measures; maintains a register of operators; controls licit uses and final destination of substances; issues certificates for import and export; replies to pre-export notifications; confirms legitimacy of transactions; collects data on seizures and licit trade; shares information with relevant national authorities.

Curaçao

Articles 18, 16

Inspector-General of Public Health
Inspectorate of Public Health
APNA-Plaza
Building E (3rd floor)
Schouwburgweg 24-26
P.O. Box 3824
Curaçao
Tel: 599 9 466 9366
Fax: 599 9 466 9367
E-mail: peter.fontilus@gov.an

On 10 October 2010, the Netherlands Antilles officially ceased to exist. Curaçao and Sint Maarten have become two new constituent entities.

Article 12

Acting Inspector of Pharmaceutical Affairs
Inspectorate of Pharmaceutical Affairs
Inspectorate of Health, Environment and Nature
P.O. Box 3824
Curaçao
Tel: 599 9 466 9366
Fax: 599 9 466 9367
E-mail: cleopatra.hazel@curacao-gov.an

Cyprus — Chypre — Chipre

Articles 18, 16

Pharmaceutical Services
Ministry of Health
Polyfimou 15
1475 Nicosia
Cyprus
Tel: 357 22 608 608 /672/637
Fax: 357 22 608 793
Fax: 357 22 608 649
E-mail: jstelliou@phs.moh.gov.cy

Cyprus — Chypre — Chipre
(continued — suite — continuación)

Article 12

As regards legislation and coordination of administrative cooperation, please refer to entry of the European Union.

Director, Pharmaceutical Services
Ministry of Health
1475 Lefkosia (Nicosia)
Cyprus
Tel: 357 22 608 608
Tel: 357 22 608 672
Fax: 357 22 608 793
E-mail: apantelidou@phs.moh.gov.cy
E-mail: jstelliou@phs.moh.gov.cy

Licensing, registration of operators, issuing import/export authorizations for substances in Tables I and II of the 1988 Convention.

Article 12

Customs and Excise Department
Customs Headquarters
1440 Nicosia
Cyprus
Tel: 357 22 601 740
Fax: 357 302 029
E-mail: kkyriakos@customs.mof.gov.cy

Investigations and seizures.

Article 12

Drug Law Enforcement Unit (YKAN)
Police Headquarters
1478 Nicosia
Cyprus
Tel: 357 22 607 374
Fax: 357 22 607 377
E-mail: lmama@police.gov.cy

Czech Republic — République tchèque — República Checa

Articles 18, 16

Ministry of Health of the Czech Republic
Inspectorate of Narcotic Drugs and Psychotropic
  Substances
Palackeho Namesti 4,
P.O. Box 81
128 01 Prague 2
Czech Republic
Tel: 420 2 2497 2710
Fax: 420 2 2491 5979
E-mail: opl@mzcr.cz

Article 12

As regards legislation and coordination of administrative cooperation, please refer to entry of the European Union.

Head, Inspectorate of Narcotic Drugs and Psychotropic
  Substances
Ministry of Health
Palackého nám. 4
P.O. Box 81
12801 Prague
Czech Republic
Tel: 420 2 2497 2710
Fax: 420 2 2491 5979
E-mail: opl@mzcr.cz

Authority responsible to issue pre-export notifications in respect of article 12, paragraph 10.

Democratic People's Republic of Korea — République populaire démocratique de Corée — República Popular Democrática de Corea

Articles 18, 16

Ministry of Public Health
Sochang-dong
Central District
Pyongyang
Democratic People's Republic of Korea
Tel: 850 2 421 4238
E-mail: bogonmoph@co.chesin.com

Article 12(*)

The Minister for Public Health
Ministry of Public Health
Pyongyang
Democratic People's Republic of Korea
Tel: 850 2 381 4410

Democratic Republic of the Congo - République démocratique du Congo - República Democrática del Congo

Articles 18, 16

Directeur, Direction de la pharmacie, médicaments et
Plantes médicinales
Ministère de la santé
B. P. 11.998
Kinshasa 1
République démocratique du Congo
Tel: 243 12 33291
Fax: 243 12 33709

Article 12(*)

Directeur, Chef des services pharmaceutiques
Ministère de la santé publique
B.P. 11.998
Kinshasa 1
République démocratique du Congo
Tel: 243 12 33291

Denmark — Danemark — Dinamarca

Articles 18, 16

Danish Medicines Agency
Axel Heides Gade 1
DK-2300 Copenhagen S
Denmark
Tel: 45 44889595
E-mail: dkma@dkma.dk

Article 12

As regards legislation and coordination of administrative cooperation, please refer to entry of the European Union.

National Danish Customs and Tax Administration
Compliance - Customs
External Relations
8 B, Sluseholmen
DK 2450 Copenhagen SV
Denmark
Tel: 45 4098 2949
Tel: 45 2013 7040
Fax: 45 7237 2917
E-mail: jorn.sorensen@skat.dk

Overall coordination and control of precursors, legal matters, licensing, registration of operators, export authorization, investigation, manufacture and internal trade, etc.

Djibouti

Articles 18, 16

Inspecteur de la pharmacie
Inspection de la pharmacie
Ministère de la santé publique
B.P. 44
Djibouti
Tel: 253 353 988

Article 12

Commissaire central de Police
Commissariat central de Djibouti
B.P. 54
Djibouti
Tel: 253 350 175

Dominica — Dominique

Article 18

Chief Medical Officer
Ministry of Health
4th Floor
Government Headquarters
Roseau
Dominica
West Indies
Tel: 1 767 266 3521
Tel: 1 767 266 3260
Fax: 1 767 448 6086
E-mail: johnsond@dominica.gov.dm

Article 16

Chief Pharmacist, Central Medical Stores
Ministry of Health and Environment
Government Headquarters
Goodwill
Roseau
Dominica
West Indies
Tel: 1 767 448 2060
Fax: 1 767 448 4882
E-mail: cms@cwdom.dm

Article 12

Chief Medical Officer
Ministry of Health
4th Floor
Government Headquarters
Kennedy Avenue
Roseau
Dominica
West Indies
Tel: 1 767 266 3260
Tel: 1 767 448 3521
Fax: 1 767 448 6086
E-mail: johnsond@dominica.gov.dm

Dominican Republic — République dominicaine — República Dominicana

Articles 18, 16

Ministerio de Salud Pública y Asistencia Social
Ave. Tiradentes Esq. San Cristóbal
Ensanche La Fe
Santo Domingo, Distrito Nacional
República Dominicana
Tel: 1 809 541 3121

Article 12

Dirección Nacional de Control de Drogas
Ministerio de Salud Pública y Asistencia Social
Sección de Químicos y Precursores
Apartado Postal No. 1344
Santo Domingo
República Dominicana
Tel: 1 809 221 4166 1242
Fax: 1 809 682 5839
E-mail: sespas@codetel.net.do

Article 12(*)

Presidente
Consejo Nacional de Drogas
Av. Mexico Oficinas Gubernamentales
Bloque "C", 1er Piso, Distrito Nacional
Santo Domingo
Dominican Republic
Tel: 1 809 221 4747
Tel: 1 809 689 3316
Tel: 1 809 689 3316
Fax: 1 809 221 8019
E-mail: fidiasf@yahoo.com
E-mail: javier.indhira@gmail.com

Ecuador — Equateur

Articles 18, 16

Secretaría Ejecutiva, Consejo Nacional de Control de
Sustancias Estupefacientes y Psicotrópicas (CONSEP)
Av. 12 de octubre N23-99 y Wilson
Quito
Ecuador
Tel: 593 2 250 6068
Tel: 593 2 222 1829
Tel: 593 2 250 6225
Fax: 593 2 256 4717
Fax: 593 2 290 4788
E-mail: secretariaejecutiva@consep.gov.ec

Article 12

Secretaría Ejecutiva, Consejo Nacional de Control de
Sustancias Estupefacientes y Psicotrópicas (CONSEP)
General Robles E-4-54 y Rio Amazonas
Quito
Ecuador
Tel: 593 2 222 1829
Fax: 593 2 256 4717
E-mail: secretariaejecutiva@consep.gov.ec
E-mail: jofre.jimenez@prevenciondrogas.gob.ec

Egypt — Egypte — Egipto

Articles 18, 16

Central Administration for Pharmaceutical Affairs (CAPA)
Ministry of Health and Population
21 Abdelaziz Al Saud
Manyal Elroda
Cairo
Egypt
Tel: 20 2 236 40368
Tel: 20 2 236 48046
Fax: 20 2 236 4194
E-mail: mostafacapa@hotmail.co.uk

Article 12

Director, Central Administration for Pharmaceutical
   Affairs
Narcotic Control Department
Ministry of Health and Population
21, Abdelaziz Al Saud Street
Manyal Elroda
Cairo
Egypt
Tel: 202 2364 0368
Tel: 202 2368 4288
Tel: 202 2364 8769
Fax: 202 2368 4194
E-mail: Narcotics@Eda.mohealth.gov.eg
E-mail: mostafacapa@hotmail.co.uk

Responsible for licensing, registration of operators,
issuing import/export authorizations for substances in
Table I and /or Table II; controlled deliveries, control,
inspection and statistics.

Article 12

Ministry of Interior
Anti-Narcotics General Administration
6 Shafik Street Abbasia
P.O. Box 11517
Cairo
Egypt
Tel: 20 2 268 38685
Tel: 20 2 268 38683
Fax: 20 2 268 23840

El Salvador

Articles 18, 16

Dirección Nacional de Medicamentos
Boulevard Merliot y Avenida Jayaque
Edificio El Gran Bazar, Nivel 4
Urbanización Jardines del Volcán
Santa Tecla
El Salvador
Tel: 503 2247 6000
Fax: 503 2247 6099
E-mail: jose.coto@medicamentos.gob.sv

Article 12(*)

Director
Dirección Nacional de Medicamentos
Edificio Gran Bazar, Avenida Jayaque
Colonia Jardines de La Libertad
Santa Tecla, La Libertad
El Salvador
Tel: 503 2522 5000
Fax: 503 2522 5075
E-mail: dirección.ejecutiva@medicamentos.gob.sv
E-mail: jose.coto@medicamentos.gob.sv

Equatorial Guinea — Guinée équatoriale — Guinea Ecuatorial

Articles 18, 16

Ministerio de Sanidad y Medio Ambiente
Malabo
Guinea Ecuatorial
Tel: 240 93550
Fax: 240 92397

Article 12(*)

Jefe Farmacéutico, Servicios Centrales de Farmacia
Ministerio de Sanidad
Malabo
Guinea Ecuatorial
Tel: 240 92397 2686
Fax: 240 92397

Eritrea — Erythrée

Articles 18, 16

Director-General, Department of Regulatory Services
Ministry of Health
P.O. Box 212
Asmara
Eritrea
Tel: 291 1 125 367
Tel: 291 1 122 336
Fax: 291 1 122 899
E-mail: asgedomm@moh.gov.er

Article 12

Director-General, Department of Pharmaceutical
   Services
Ministry of Health
P.O. Box 212
Asmara
Eritrea
Tel: 291 1 125 367
Tel: 291 1 122 336
Fax: 291 1 122 899

Controls importation, manufacture and distribution of drugs, including narcotic drugs and psychotropic substances.

Estonia — Estonie

Articles 18, 16

State Agency of Medicines
Nooruse Str. 1
50411 Tartu
Estonia
Tel: 372 7 374 140
Fax: 372 7 374 142
E-mail: eda.lopato@ravimiamet.ee
Web: www.ravimiamet.ee

Article 12

As regards legislation and coordination of administrative cooperation, please refer to entry of the European Union.

Head, Bureau of Import, Narcotic Drugs and
   Psychotropic Substances
State Agency of Medicines
1 Nooruse Str.
50411 Tartu
Estonia
Tel: 372 7 374 140
Fax: 372 7 374 142
E-mail: Eda.Lopato@sam.ee
E-mail: sam@sam.ee

Regulation of the manufacture and use of drugs.

Article 12

As regards legislation and coordination of administrative cooperation, please refer to entry of the European Union.

Ministry of Health
Vismari 15
0031 Tallinn
Estonia
Tel: 372 2 451 783
Fax: 372 2 440 869

Addiction control centre coordinating efforts against the abuse of drugs.

Estonia — Estonie
(continued — suite — continuación)

Article 12

As regards legislation and coordination of administrative cooperation, please refer to entry of the European Union.

Department Head
Ministry of Trade
Kiriku 2
Tallinn
Estonia
Tel: 372 2 691 486
Fax: 372 2 450 540

Ethiopia — Ethiopie — Etiopía

Articles 18, 16

Drug Administration and Control Authority
P.O. Box 5681
Addis Ababa
Ethiopia
Tel: 251 11 552 4122 /18
Fax: 251 11 552 1392
E-mail: daca@ethionet.et

Article 12

Director-General
Ethiopian Food, Medicine and Health Care Administration
and
Control Authority
P.O. Box 5681
Addis Ababa
Ethiopia
Tel: 251 1552 4123
Tel: 251 1552 4122
Fax: 251 1552 1392
E-mail: regulatory@fmhaca.gov.et

Issuing of import/export authorization certificates.

Falkland Islands (Malvinas) –
Îles Falkland (Malvinas) –
Islas Malvinas (Falkland Islands)

Articles 18, 16

King Edward VII Memorial Hospital
Port Stanley
Falkland Islands (Malvinas)
Tel: 500 27214
Fax: 500 27416

Article 12

Chief Medical Officer, Medical Department
King Edward VII Memorial Hospital
Port Stanley
Falkland Islands (Malvinas)
Tel: 500 28000
Fax: 500 28002
E-mail: CMO@kemh.gov.fk

Regulation of national controls, issuance of import authorizations.

Article 12

Royal Falkland Islands Police
Police Station
Ross Road
Stanley
Tel: 500 28100
Fax: 500 28110
E-mail: admin@police.gov.fk

Enforcement of national controls, investigation of violations.

Article 12

Customs and Immigration Department
3 H. Jones Road
Stanley
Falkland Islands
Tel: 500 27340
Fax: 500 27342
E-mail: admin@customs.gov.lk

Enforcement of national controls, investigation of violations, regulation of import authorizations

Fiji — Fidji

Articles 18, 16

Permanent Secretary for Health
Ministry of Health Department
Government Building, P.O. Box 2223
Suva
Fiji
Tel: 679 306 177
Fax: 679 306 163

Article 12

The Chief Pharmacist
Fiji Pharmaceutical and Biomedical Services (FPBS)
  Center
Ministry of Health
GPO Box 106
Suva
Fiji
Tel: 679 338 8000 extension 113
Fax: 679 338 8003
E-mail: Muaniamma.gounder@govnet.gov.fj

Article 12(*)

Permanent Secretary for Health
Ministry of Health
P.O. Box 2223
Government Buildings
Suva
Fiji
Tel: 679 322 1500
Fax: 679 330 6177
E-mail: SSaketa@health.gov.fj.fj

Finland — Finlande — Finlandia

Articles 18, 16

Finnish Medicines Agency, Fimea
P.O. Box 55
00034 Fimea
Finland
Tel: 358 29 522 3341
Fax: 358 29 522 3002
E-mail: registry@fimea.fi

Article 12

As regards legislation and coordination of administrative cooperation, please refer to entry of the European Union.

Finnish Medicines Agency (Fimea)
Inspectorate
Mannerheimintie 103b
P. O. Box 55
00301 Helsinki
Finland
Tel: 358 9 473 341
Fax: 358 9 473 342 67
E-mail: registry@fimea.fi
E-mail: precursors@fimea.fi

France — Francia

Articles 18, 16

Agence nationale de sécurité du médicament et des
   produits de santé
143-147, Boulevard Anatole France
93285 Saint-Denis
France
Tel: 33 1 5587 3633
Fax: 33 1 5587 3592
E-mail: aldine.fabreguettes@ansm.sante.fr
E-mail: marie-anne.courne@ansm.sante.fr
E-mail: elena.salazar@ansm.sante.fr

Article 12

As regards legislation and coordination of administrative cooperation, please refer to entry of the European Union.

Directeur général
Agence Nationale de Sécurité du Médicament
   et des Produits de Santé (ANSM)
Département stupéfiants et psychotropes
143-147 boulevard Anatole France
93285 SAINT DENIS CEDEX
FRANCE
Tel: 33 1 55 87 35 91
Tel: 33 1 55 87 35 93
Fax: 33 1 55 87 35 92
E-mail: aldine.fabreguettes@ansm.sante.fr
E-mail: marie-anne.courne@ansm.sante.fr
E-mail: elena.salazar@ansm.sante.fr

Monitoring of 1-phenyl-2-propanone and lysergic acid.

Article 12

As regards legislation and coordination of administrative cooperation, please refer to entry of the European Union.

Mission Nationale de Contrôle des Précurseurs
   Chimiques (MNCPC)
Direction Générale des Enterprises (DGE)
67 rue Barbès 94201 Ivry sur Seine Cedex
France
Tel: 33 1 79 84 31 69
Fax: 33 1 79 84 36 37
E-mail: mncpc@finances.gouv.fr

Monitors all Table I and II substances except 1-phenyl-2 propanone and lysergic acid. Registration and approval of companies. Export and import authorizations.

Article 12

As regards legislation and coordination of administrative cooperation, please refer to entry of the European Union.

Direction nationale du renseignement et des enquêtes
   douanières (DNRED)
DRD - Direction du Renseignement Douanier
Observatoire des précurseurs
2 mail Monique Maunoury
TSA 10313, 94853 IVRSUR-SEINE cedex
France
Tel: 33 1 49 23 36 36
Fax: 33 1 49 23 39 23
Fax: 33 1 49 23 39 22

Control and investigation.

France — Francia
(continued — suite — continuación)

Article 12

As regards legislation and coordination of administrative cooperation, please refer to entry of the European Union.

Office Central pour la Répression du Traffic Illicite des Stupéfiants (OCTRIS)
101, rue des Trois Fontanot
92000 Nanterre
France
Tel: 33 1 40 97 80 40
Tel: 33 1 49 27 40 21
Fax: 33 1 47 21 03 20

Control and investigation.

French Polynesia – Polynésie française – Polinesia Francesa

Articles 18, 16

Direction de la santé
B.P. 611
98713 Papeete
Polynésie française
Tel: 689 460 002
Fax: 689 460 074
E-mail: secretariat@sante.gov.pf

Article 12

Mission Nationale de Contrôle des Précurseurs Chimiques (MNCPC)
Direction Générale des Entreprises (DGE)
67 rue Barbès 94201 Ivry sur Seine Cedex
France
Tel: 33 1 7984 3169
Fax: 33 1 7984 3637
E-mail: mncpc@finances.gouv.fr

Gabon — Gabón

Article 12(*)

Ministère de la santé publique et de la population
Inspection générale de la santé publique
Division Pharmacie
B.P. 2279
Libreville
Gabon
Tel: 241 764 530
Fax: 241 764 534

(Article not specified)

Ministère de la santé publique et de la population
Section pharmacie d'approvisionnement
B.P. 295
Libreville
Gabon
Tel: 241 764 708
Fax: 241 722 407

Gambia — Gambie

Articles 18, 16

Medicines Board
Department of State for Health
Banjul
Gambia
Tel: 220 225 374
Fax: 220 225 873

Article 12

Chief Pharmacist
National Pharmaceutical Services
Near Kotu Power Station
Ministry of Health & Social Welfare
Banjul
The Gambia
Tel: 220 4466 302
Tel: 220 4460 068
Fax: 220 4466 303
E-mail: mjkaira@moh.gov.gm

Georgia — Géorgie

Articles 18, 16

Ministry of Labour, Health and Social Affairs of Georgia (LEPL)
State Regulation Agency for Medical Activities
Ak. Tsereteli Avenue 144
0159 Tbilisi
Georgia
Tel: 995 32 272 5081
E-mail: drugcontrol@moh,gov.ge

Article 12

Chief
Ministry of Labour, Health and Social Affairs of Georgia
LEPL State Regulation Agency for Medical Activities
AK. Tsereteli Avenue 144
0119 Tbilisi
Georgia
Tel: 995 32 272 5081
E-mail: drugcontrol@moh.gov.ge

Implementation of provisions of article 12 of the 1988 Convention.

Germany — Allemagne — Alemania

Articles 18, 16

Federal Institute for Drugs and Medical Devices
Federal Opium Agency
Kurt-Georg-Kiesinger Allee 3
53175 Bonn
Germany
Tel: 49 228 20 730
Fax: 49 228 20 75210
E-mail: poststelle@BFArM.de

Article 12

As regards legislation and coordination of administrative cooperation, please refer to entry of the European Union.

Joint Customs and Police Precursor Monitoring Unit
Federal Criminal Police Office
Gemeinsame Grundstoffüberwachungsstelle
Zollkriminalamt (ZKA)/Bundeskriminalamt (BKA) beim
  Bundeskriminalamt (GÜS)
65173 Wiesbaden
Germany

Tel: 49 611 55 14888
Tel: 49 611 55 14086
Fax: 49 611 55 14093
E-mail: so22-gues@bka.bund.de

Compiles statistics on seizures and methods of diversion and illicit manufacture as found by police. Investigations. Controlled deliveries.

Article 12

As regards legislation and coordination of administrative cooperation, please refer to entry of the European Union.

Customs Criminological Office
Zollkriminalamt
Postfach 850562
51030 Köln
Germany
Tel: 49 221 672 4300
Tel: 49 221 67 24301
Fax: 49 221 67 24500 (Central)
Fax: 49 221 67 24374
E-mail: III4@zka.bfinv.de

Coordinates customs-monitoring of import, export and transit; coordinates investigations of violations; compiles statistics on methods of diversion and illicit manufacture.

Article 12

As regards legislation and coordination of administrative cooperation, please refer to entry of the European Union.

Federal Institute for Drugs and Medical Devices
Federal Opium Agency
Kurt-Georg-Kiesinger-Allee 3
53175 Bonn
Germany
Tel: 49 228 20 730
Fax: 49 228 20 75210

Licenses and registers operators, issues export authorizations, suspends suspicious exports, receives and confirms export documents.

Ghana

Article 18

Narcotics Control Board
P.M.B., Cantonments
Accra
Ghana
Tel: 233 217 61 072
Tel: 233 217 61 028
Fax: 233 302 176 1618
E-mail: info@nacob.gov.gh

Article 12

Executive Secretary
Narcotics Control Board
Private Mail Bag, Cantonments
Accra
Ghana
Tel: 233 302 761 065
Tel: 233 302 761 028
Fax: 233 302 761 518
E-mail: info@nacob.gov.gh

Responsible for registration of both pharmaceutical and mining (industrial), issuing import and export authorizations for substances in Table I and/or Table II , investigations of violations and controlled deliveries

Article 12

Chief Executive Officer
Food and Drugs Authority
P.O. Box CT2783 Cantonments
Accra
Ghana
Tel: 233 302 233 200
Tel: 233 302 235 100
Fax: 233 302 225 502
Fax: 233 302 229 794
E-mail: fda@fdaghana.gov.gh
Web: www.fdaghana.gov.gh

Responsible for licensing, registration of pharmaceutical importers, issuing import and export authorizations for substances in Table I and/or Table II, investigations of violations and controlled deliveries.

Article 12

Environmental Protection Agency
P.O. Box MB 326
Ministries Post Office
Accra
Ghana
Tel: 233 302 662 465
Tel: 233 302 667 524
Tel: 233 302 664 698
Tel: 233 302 664 697
Fax: 233 302 662 690
E-mail: info@epa.gov.gh

Responsible for licensing, issuing import and export authorizations for substances in Table I and/or Table II, investigations of violations and controlled deliveries.

Gibraltar

Articles 18, 16

Government of Gibraltar
6 Convent Place
Gibraltar
Tel: 350 70071
Fax: 350 76396
E-mail: cs@gibraltar.gov.gi

Greece — Grèce — Grecia

Articles 18, 16

Ministry of Health and Social Solidarity
Directorate of Medicines and Pharmacies
Division of Narcotic Drugs
17 Aristotelous Str.
10187 Athens
Greece
Tel: 30 210 523 0703
Tel: 30 210 522 5301
Fax: 30 210 522 7360
E-mail: farmaka@mohaw.gr

Article 12

As regards legislation and coordination of administrative cooperation, please refer to entry of the European Union.

General Chemical State Laboratories
Division of Drugs
Department of Narcotics
Ministry of Finance
16 An. Tsocha Street
11521 Athens
Greece
Tel: 30 210 646 4246
Tel: 30 210 642 8211 Ext. 232
Tel: 30 210 642 8211 Ext. 233
Fax: 30 210 646 5123

Registering companies for substances listed in category 2 and 3 of the EEC regulation.

Article 12

As regards legislation and coordination of administrative cooperation, please refer to entry of the European Union.

Directorate General of Customs and Excise Duties
Ministry of Finance
33rd Division of Custom Controls
Section B
"Drugs and Arms Enforcement"
10. Kar Servias Street
10184 Athens
Greece
Tel: 30 210 725 9328
Fax: 30 210 322 5192
E-mail: rilod33b@otenet.gr

Licensing, registration, export authorization and controlled deliveries.

Article 12

As regards legislation and coordination of administrative cooperation, please refer to entry of the European Union.

National Organization of Medicines
Mesogion 284
Holargos
Greece
Tel: 30 210 654 5196
Tel: 30 210 654 5530
Fax: 30 210 654 9591

Licensing companies for substances listed in category 1 of the EEC regulation.

Grenada — Grenade — Granada

Articles 18, 16

The Chief Medical Officer
Ministry of Health
Ministerial Complex
Botanical Gardens
St. Georges
Grenada
Tel: 1 473 440 3485
Fax: 1 473 440 4127
E-mail: Min-healthgrenada@caribsurf.com

Article 12

Chief Analytical Chemist
Grenada Produce Chemist Laboratory
Tanteen
St. Georges
Grenada
Tel: 1 473 440 3273
Fax: 1 473 440 4191

Narcotics testing; pesticides, registration and licensing.

Guam

See information immediately under United States of America, **Articles 18, 16**

Guatemala

Articles 18, 16

Departamento de Control de Medicamentos
Sección de Sicotrópicos, Estupefacientes e
   Importaciones
3a calle final, 2.20
Colonia Valles de Vista
Hermosa Zona 15,
Ciudad de Guatemala
Guatemala
Tel: 502 2 365 6255-60
Fax: 502 2 365 6255-60
E-mail: seccionsicotropicosguate@yahoo.com

Article 12(*)

Secretaría Ejecutiva, Comisión contra las Adicciones y el
   Tráfico Ilícito de Drogas (SECCATID)
Vicepresidencia de la República
2a Calle 1-00 Zona 10
Ciudad de Guatemala
Guatemala
Tel: 502 2361 2620
Tel: 502 2331 1781
Fax: 502 2331 0372
E-mail: seccatid@gua.net

Verification of legitimacy of transaction.

Article 12(*)

Jefa, Sección de Psicotrópicos,Estupefacientes
Importaciones y Exportaciones
Ministerio de Salud Pública y Asistencia Social
3a. Calle final 2-10,Valles de Vista Hermosa, Zona 15
Ciudad de Guatemala
Guatemala
Tel: 502 2365 6255-6260
Fax: 502 2365 6255-6260 extn 112
E-mail: drcpfacontrolados@gmail.com

Responsible for licensing, registration of operators, issuing import/export authorizations for substances in Table I and Table II substances.

Guinea — Guinée

Article 18

Direction nationale des pharmacies et laboratoires
Ministère de la santé publique
BP 585
Conakry
Guinée
Tel: 224 30 45 20 28
Fax: 224 30 45 20 50

Article 16

Ministère de la santé publique
Conakry
Guinée
Tel: 224 60 29 70 71
Fax: 224 30 45 20 50
E-mail: harirata@yahoo.fr

Article 12

Directeur national de la pharmacie et des laboratoires
Directeur national de la pharmacie
   et des laboratoires (DNPL)
Ministère de la Santé et de l'Hygiène Publique
B.P. 1490
Conakry
Guinée
Tel: 224 6873 3804
Tel: 224 6460 1001
E-mail: dafelaka@hotmail.fr
E-mail: dafelaka@yahoo.fr
E-mail: drsouare_kabine@yahoo.fr

Issuing of import/export authorizations. Furnishing statistics on imports, exports and consumption.

Guinea-Bissau — Guinée-Bissau

Articles 18, 16

Ministère de la santé publique
Direction des services pharmaceutiques
Boîte postale 50
Bissau
Guinée-Bissau
Tel: 245 212 148

Article 12(*)

Le Secrétaire général
Ministère de la santé
Cabinet de ministre
Av. Unidade Africana
Boîte postale 50
Bissau
Guinée-Bissau
Tel: 245 204 438
Fax: 245 202 237
E-mail: gminsapgov@hotmail.com

Guyana

Articles 18, 16

Government Analyst, Food and Drug Department
Mudlot, Kingston
P.O. Box 1019
Georgetown
Guyana
Tel: 592 226 3711
Fax: 592 225 4249
E-mail: fooddrug@networksgy.com

Article 12(*)

Government Analyst, Food and Drug Department
Institute of Applied Science and Technology (IAST)
   Building
University of Guyana, Turkeyen Campus
Turkeyen
East Coast Demerara
Guyana
Tel: 592 222 8857
Tel: 592 222 8859
Fax: 592 222 8856

Haiti — Haïti — Haití

Articles 18, 16

Direction centrale de pharmacie et de contrôle des
   Substances chimiques (DCP/CSC)
Ministère de la santé publique et de la population
Palais des Ministères
Port-au-Prince
Haïti
Tel: 509 245 5835
Tel: 509 228 2522

Article 12

Directrice
Direction de la pharmacie du medicament
   et de la medecine Traditionnelle (DPM/MT)
Ministère de la Santé Publique et de la Population
Angle Avenue Maïs Gaté et Rue Jacques Roumain #1
PORT-AU-PRINCE
Haïti
Tel: 509 2226 9258
E-mail: fjoseph@mspp.gouv.ht
E-mail: dpmmt@mspp.gouv.ht

Holy See — Saint-Siège — Santa Sede

Articles 18, 16

Pontifical Council for Pastoral Assistance to Health Care
   Workers
Via della Conciliazione N.3
00193 Rome
Italy
Tel: 39 06 6988 3138
Tel: 39 06 6988 4720
Fax: 39 06 6988 3139

Articles 18, 16

General Secretariat of the Governorate
00120 Vatican City State
Holy See
Tel: 39 06 6988 3158
Tel: 39 06 6988 4459
Fax: 39 06 6988 5299

Honduras

Articles 18, 16

Direccion General de Regulacion Sanitaria
Secretaría de Salud
Edificio Anexo No. 1
Avenida Máximo Jerez
esquina opuesta Farmacia Regis Centro
Primer Piso
Tegucigalpa, MEC
Honduras
Tel: 504 237 1141
Fax: 504 237 2726
E-mail: codexhonduras@hotmail.com

Article 12

Secretaría de Estado en el Despacho de Salud
Sección de Control de Estupefacientes
  y otras Drogas Peligrosas
Departamento de Farmacia
3a calle y 4a avenida
Tegucigalpa, M.D.C.
Honduras
Tel: 504 2220 7006
Tel: 504 2237 1141 ext. 38
Fax: 504 2237 2726
E-mail: drogasdgrs@gmail.com

Issues import authorizations.

Article 12

Jefe, Departamento Valoración Aduanera
Dirección General de Aduanas
Edificio Plaza Morazán
Contíguo a Banco Futuro, 11 Piso
Tegucigalpa, M.D.C.
Honduras
Tel: 504 238 2541
Tel: 504 238 2538
Fax: 504 238 2621

Hong Kong Special Administrative Region (SAR) of China – Région administrative spéciale (RAS) de Hong Kong (Chine) – Región Administrativa Especial (RAE) de Hong Kong de China

Articles 18, 16

Chief Pharmacist (2)
Drug Office Department of Health
3/F, Public Health Laboratory Centre
382 Nam Cheong Street
Kowloon
Hong Kong SAR of China
Tel: 852 2319 8671
Fax: 852 2319 6303
E-mail: frankchan@dh.gov.hk

Article 12

Commissioner for Narcotics
Narcotics Division
Attn: Assistant Secretary for Security (Narcotics)
Narcotics Division
Security Bureau
Queensway Government Offices
High Block, 30th floor
66 Queensway
Hong Kong SAR of China
Tel: 852 2867 2755
Fax: 852 2521 7761
Fax: 852 2810 1790

Article 12

Commissioner of Customs and Excise, Head of
  Controlled Chemicals Group
Hong Kong Customs and Excise Department
21/F Customs Headquarters Building
222 Java Road, North Point
Hong Kong SAR of China
Tel: 852 3759 2822
Fax: 852 2541 1016
E-mail: sai_kwong_leung@customs.gov.hk

For technical matters.

Hungary — Hongrie — Hungría

Articles 18, 16

Health Registration and Training Center
National Drugs Control Department
Zrínyi utca. 3
1051 Budapest
Hungary
Tel: 36 1 235 7970
Fax: 36 1 311 0063
E-mail: narcotic@enkk.hu

Article 12

As regards legislation and coordination of administrative
cooperation, please refer to entry of the European Union.

Hungarian Trade Licensing Office
Trade Authority
Németvölgyi út 37-39
H-1534 Budapest, BKKP
P.O.B. 919
Hungary
Tel: 36 1 4585 514
Tel: 36 1 4585 504
Fax: 36 1 4585 828
E-mail: keo@mkeh.gov.hu

Licensing and registration, issuing export and import
authorizations, control and monitoring of licit trade.

Article 12

As regards legislation and coordination of administrative cooperation, please refer to entry of the European Union.

National Tax and Customs Administration
Directorate General for Criminal Affairs
Hajnóczy u. 7-9.
H - 1122 Budapest
Hungary
Tel: 361 456 8102
Fax: 361 456 8148
E-mail: bfig@nav.gov.hu

Control and monitoring of legal export/import, investigations of diversion.

Article 12

As regards legislation and coordination of administrative cooperation, please refer to entry of the European Union.

Hungarian National Police Headquarters
General Directorate for Criminal Investigations
Criminal Department
Criminal Division
Teve u. 4-6
1139 Budapest
Hungary
Tel: 36 1 443 5513
Fax: 36 1 443 5676
E-mail: drcsako@orfk.police.hu

Investigation of diversion, law enforcement.

Iceland — Islande — Islandia

Articles 18, 16

Icelandic Medicines Agency (IMA)
Vinlandsleið 14
113 Reykjavik
Iceland
Tel: 354 520 2100
Fax: 354 561 2170
E-mail: ima@ima.is

Article 12

Directorate of Customs
Tryggvagata 19
101 Reykjavik
Iceland
Tel: 354 560 0300
E-mail: customs@customs.is

Controlled deliveries.

Article 12

The National Commissioner of Icelandic Police
Skúlagata 21
101 Reykjavik
Iceland
Tel: 354 444 2500
Fax: 354 444 2501
Fax: rls@rls.is

Investigations of violations.

Article 12(*)

Icelandic Medicines Agency
Vinlandsleið 14
113 Reykjavik
Iceland
Tel: 354 520 2100
Fax: 354 561 2170
E-mail: ima@ima.is

Responsible for licensing, issuing import/export authorizations for substances in Table I and/or Table II.

India — Inde

Articles 18, 16

Central Bureau of Narcotics
Ministry of Finance
19, The Mall
Morar
Gwalior 474006
Madhya Pradesh
India
Tel: 91 751 236 8996
Tel: 91 751 236 8997
Tel: 91 751 236 8121
Fax: 91 751 236 8111
Fax: 91 751 236 8577
E-mail: narcom@sancharnet.in

Articles 18, 16

Director General, Narcotics Control Bureau
Ministry of Home Affairs
Department of Internal Security
West Block No. 1, Wing No. 5
Puram
New Delhi 110066
India
Tel: 91 11 2617 2089
Fax: 91 11 2610 5747
E-mail: dg-ncb@nic.in

Mandated to discharge the obligations under articles 18 and 16.

Article 12

Director-General, Narcotics Control Bureau
Ministry of Home Affairs
West Block No. 1, Wing V
R.K. Puram
New Delhi 110066
India
Tel: 91 11 2617 2089
Fax: 91 11 2610 5747
E-mail: dg-ncb@nic.in

To regulate or enforce national controls over precursors and essential chemicals.

Article 12

Narcotics Commissioner
Central Bureau of Narcotics
Ministry of Finance
Department of Revenue
19, The Mall Road
Morar
Gwalior 474006
Madhya Pradesh
India
Tel: 91 751 236 8997
Tel: 91 751 236 8121
Tel: 91 751 236 8996
Fax: 91 751 236 8577
Fax: 91 751 236 8111
E-mail: narcommr@cbn.nic.in
E-mail: narcom@sancharnet.in

Issuance of "No Objection Certificate" in respect of export and import of precursor chemicals and furnishing of information to the importing country/by the exporting country.

Indonesia — Indonésie

Articles 18, 16

Director-General, Pharmaceutical Services and Medical
  Devices
Ministry of Health
Jl. Hr. Rasuna Said Blok X5
Kavling No. 4-9
Jakarta 12950
Indonesia
Tel: 62 21 520 1590

Article 12

Director General, Pharmaceutical Services and Medical
  Equipment Division
Department of Health
Jalan H.R. Rasuna Said Block X5 kav. 4-9
Kuningan, Jakarta 12950
Indonesia
Tel: 62 21 520 1590
Tel: 62 21 521 4876
Fax: 62 21 529 64838

Article 12

Executive Director, National Narcotics Board (BNN)
  (Badan Narkotika Nasional (BNN))
Jl. MT. Haryono No. 11 Cawang
Jakarta Timur
Indonesia
Tel: 62 21 8087 1567
Tel: 62 21 8087 1566
Fax: 62 21 8087 1591
Fax: 62 21 8087 1632
Fax: 62 21 8088 5225
Fax: 62 21 8087 1593
Fax: 62 21 8087 1592
E-mail: info@bnn.go.id

Overall coordination. Collection of seizure data.

Article 12

Criminal Investigation Corps
Narcotics Directorate (Direktorat Reserse Narkoba,
  Korserse Polri)
Jl. Trunojoyo No. 3, Kebayoran Baru
Jakarta Selatan
Indonesia
Tel: 62 21 739 2461
Fax: 62 21 739 2461

Article 12

Directorate of Import & Export, Directorate General of
  Foreign Trade
Ministry of Trade
Jl. Ridwan Rais No. 5
Jakarta Pusat 10110
Indonesia
Tel: 62 21 385 8171 ext. 35900, 1145, 1176
Fax: 62 21 385 8194
E-mail: import@kemendag.go.id

Issuing import license for precursor non pharmaceutical

Iran (Islamic Republic of) —
Iran (République islamique d') —
Irán (República Islámica de)

Articles 18, 16

Drug Control Headquarters and Ministry of
  Health Treatment and Medical Education
Fakhr-e-Razi St. Enghelab Ave.
P.O. Box 13145-719
Tehran
Iran (Islamic Republic of)
Tel: 98 21 6646 6939
Tel: 98 21 6646 6930
Fax: 98 21 6646 9142

Article 12

Director General, Division of Pharmaceutical and
   Narcotic Affairs (DPNA)
Ministry of Health and Medical Education
Fakhr-e-Razi
Tehran
Iran (Islamic Republic of)
Tel: 98 21 6640 5591
Tel: 98 21 6646 6939
Tel: 98 21 6646 6930
Fax: 98 21 6646 9142
E-mail: h.rahimi@fdo.gov.ir

Issue of import certificates for substances in Tables I and
II of the 1988 Convention. Replies to inquiries about
legitimacy of transactions.

Article 12

Secretary, Drug Control Headquarters
No. 32 North Naft Ave, Dastjerdi St.
Modarres Highway, P.O. Box 19395-7341
Tehran, Islamic Republic of Iran
Tel: 98 21 2290 1220
Fax: 98 21 2290 1221
E-mail: info@dchq.ir

Law enforcement and investigation.

Iraq

Articles 18, 16

Directorate of Technical Affairs
Ministry of Health
Bab Al-Mu'adham
Maidan Square
P.O. Box 14188
Baghdad
Iraq
Tel: 964 1 415 8401
E-mail: pharmacydepmoh@yahoo.com

Article 12

Director General
Directorate of Technical Affairs
Pharmacy Department
Narcotic Drugs Psychotropics
   & Controlled Substances
Management Section, Ministry of Health
P.O. Box 14188
Baghdad
Iraq
Tel: 964 1 4158401/9 extn 1513
E-mail: moh.pharm@yahoo.com
E-mail: pharmacydepmoh@gmail.com

Ireland — Irlande — Irlanda

Articles 18, 16

Controlled Drugs Unit, Department of Health
Hawkins House
Hawkins Street
Dublin 2
Ireland
Tel: 353 1 635 4000
Fax: 353 1 635 4001
E-mail: controlled_drugs@health.gov.ie
E-mail: siobhan_kennan@health.gov.ie

Article 12(*)

As regards legislation and coordination of administrative
cooperation, please refer to entry of the European Union.

Assistant Secretary
Department of Health
Hawkins House
Hawkins Street
Dublin 2
Ireland
Tel: 353 1 635 4000
Fax: 353 1 635 4443
E-mail: paul_barron@health.gov.ie

Isle of Man - Île de Man – Isla de Man

Articles 18, 16

Department of Health and Social Security
Markwell House
Market Street
Douglas
Isle of Man
British Isles IM1 2RZ
Tel: 44 1624 685 004
Fax: 44 1624 685 130
E-mail: ceo.dhss@gov.im

Israel — Israël

Articles 18, 16

Pharmaceutical Administration
Yermiahu 39 POB 1176
Jerusalem 91010
Israel
Tel: 972 2 5080273
Fax: 972 2 647 4862
E-mail: tal.lavy@moh.health.gov.il

Article 12

Head
Department of Pharmaceutical Control and
  Quality Assurance
Ministry of Health
P.O. Box 1176
Yermiahu 39 St.
Jerusalem 91010
Israel
Tel: 972 2 5080 273
Fax: 972 2 647 4862
E-mail: tal.lavy@moh.health.gov.il

Responsible for authorizing imports of ephedrine, pseudoephedrine, ergometrine, ergotamine, lysergic acid.

Article 12

The Anti-Drug Authority of Israel (ADA)
7, Kanfei Nesharim St.
Givat Shaul
P.O. Box 3985
Jerusalem 91039
Israel
Tel: 972 2 567 5911
Fax: 972 2 651 3956

Law enforcement; in particular for queries on substances not covered by the Ministry of Health.

Italy — Italie — Italia

Articles 18, 16

Central Office for Narcotic Drugs
Ministry of Health
Viale Giorgio Ribotta, 5
00144 Rome
Italy
Tel: 39 06 5994 3689
Fax: 39 06 5994 3226
E-mail: r.signorile@sanita.it

Article 12

As regards legislation and coordination of administrative cooperation, please refer to entry of the European Union.

Director
Ministry of Health
DGDMF Direzione Generale dei Dispositivi Medici
  e del Servizio Farmaceutico
Central Office of Drugs
Viale Giorgio Ribotta, 5
00144 Roma
Italy
Tel: 39 06 5994 3689
Fax: 39 06 5994 3226
E-mail: dgfdm@postacert.sanita.it
E-mail: g.apuzzo@sanita.it
E-mail: r. signorile@sanita.it
E-mail: c.romoli@sanita.it

Register of substances, import/export authorizations for substances in Table I of the 1988 Convention.

Article 12

As regards legislation and coordination of administrative cooperation, please refer to entry of the European Union.

Central Directorate for Antidrug Services
Ministry of Interior
Via Torre di Mezzavia, 9/121
0173 Rome
Italy
Tel: 39 06 4652 3000
Fax: 39 06 4652 3885
E-mail: direzione.antidroga@interno.it

Responsible for fight against diversion of chemical substances.

Jamaica — Jamaïque

Articles 18, 16

Ministry of Health
45-47 Barbados Avenue
Kingston 5
Jamaica
West Indies
Tel: 1876 633-7137
Fax: 1876 633-7433
E-mail: ClarkeCo@moh.gov.jm

Articles 18, 16

Ministry of Health
Pharmaceutical & Regulatory Affairs Department
Standards & Regulation Division
45-47 Barbados Avenue
Kingston 5
Jamaica
West Indies
Tel: 1876 633-7140
Fax: 1876 630-3630
E-mail: edwardsv@moh.gov.jm

Article 12

Chief Medical Officer, Attn: Chief Dangerous Drugs
  Inspector
Ministry of Health
Pharmaceutical and Regulatory Affairs Department
2-4 King Street
Kingston
Jamaica
Tel: 1876 922 3851
Fax: 1876 967 1629
E-mail: edwardsv@moh.gov.jm

Japan — Japon — Japón

Article 18

Compliance and Narcotics Division
Pharmaceutical and Food Safety Bureau
Ministry of Health, Labour and Welfare
2-2, 1-chome, Kasumigaseki, Chiyoda-ku
Tokyo 100 8916
Japan
Tel: 81 3 3595 2454
Fax: 81 3 3501 0034

Article 16

Narcotics Control Department, Hokkaido Regional
Bureau of Health and Welfare
1-1, Nishi 2-chome, Kita 8-jo, Kita-ku
Sapporo-shi 060 0808
Japan
Tel: 81 11 726 3131
Fax: 81 11 709 8063

Area in charge: Hokkaido

Article 16

Narcotics Control Department
Tohoku Regional Bureau of Health
  and Welfare
2-23, Hon-cho 3-chome, Aoba-ku
Sendai-shi 980 0014
Japan
Tel: 81 22 221 3701
Fax: 81 22 221 3713

Area in charge: Aomori, Iwate, Miyagi, Akita, Yamagata,
Fukushima

Article 16

Narcotics Control Department, Kanto-Shin'etsu
  Regional Bureau of Health and Welfare
2-1, Kudanminami 1-chome, Chiyoda-ku
Tokyo 102 8309
Japan
Tel: 81 3 3512 8688
Fax: 81 3 3512 8689

Area in charge: Ibaraki, Tochigi, Gunma, Saitama, Chiba,
Tokyo, Kanagawa, Yamanashi, Nagano, Niigata

Article 16

Narcotics Control Department, Tokai-Hokuriku
  Regional Bureau of Health and Welfare
5-1, Sannomaru 2-chome, Naka-ku
Nagoya-shi 460 0001
Japan
Tel: 81 52 951 6911
Fax: 81 52 951 6876

Area in charge: Shizuoka, Aichi, Mie, Gifu, Toyama,
Ishikawa

Article 16

Narcotics Control Department
Kinki Regional Bureau of Health and Welfare
1-76, Otemae 4-chome, Chuo-ku
Osaka-shi 540 0008
Japan
Tel: 81 6 6949 6336
Fax: 81 6 6949 6339

Area in charge: Fukui, Shiga, Kyoto, Osaka, Hyogo,
Nara, Wakayama

Article 16

Narcotics Control Department
Chugoku-Shikoku Regional Bureau of Health
  and Welfare
6-30, Kami-Hacchobori, Naka-ku
Hiroshima-shi 730 0012
Japan
Tel: 81 82 227 9011
Fax: 81 82 227 9174

Area in charge: Tottori, Shimane, Okayama, Hiroshima,
Yamaguti

Article 16

Narcotics Control Department
Shikoku Regional Bureau of Health and Welfare
3-33, Sunport
Takamatsu-shi 760 0019
Japan
Tel: 81 87 811 8910
Fax: 81 87 823 8810

Area in charge: Tokushima, Kagawa, Ehime, Kouchi

Article 16

Narcotics Control Department
Kyushu Regional Bureau of Health and Welfare
10-7, Hakataekihigashi 2-chome, Hakata-ku
Fukuoka-shi 812 0013
Japan
Tel: 81 92 472 2331
Fax: 81 92 472 2336

Area in charge: Fukuoka, Saga, Nagasaki, Kumamoto,
Oita, Miyazaki, Kagoshima, Okinawa

Article 12(*)

Director-General, Compliance and Narcotics Division
Pharmaceutical and Food Safety Bureau
Ministry of Health, Labour and Welfare
2-2, 1-Chome, Kasumigaseki, Chiyoda-ku
Tokyo 100 8916
Japan
Tel: 81 3 35952436
Tel: 81 3 35952454
Fax: 81 3 35010034

Article 12(*)

Director, Chemical Weapon and Materials Control Policy
    Office
Ministry of Economy, Trade and Industry
1-3-1, Kasumigaseki, Chiyoda-ku
Tokyo 100 8901
Japan
Tel: 81 3 35800937
Fax: 81 3 35807319

Only for exchange of information on export/import of acetic anhydride, acetone, anthranlic acid, ethyl ether, hydrochloric acid, methyl ethyl ketone, piperidine, potassium permanganate, sulphuric acid and toluene.

Jordan — Jordanie — Jordania

Articles 18, 16

Jordan Food and Drug Administration (JFDA)
Shafa Badran Marj Alfaras
P.O. Box 811951
Amman, P.C 11181
Jordan
Tel: 962 6 563 2000
Fax: 962 6 523 0376
Fax: 962 6 510 5893
Fax: 962 6 510 5916
E-mail: Info@jfda.jo

Article 12

General Director, Jordan Food and Drug Administration
P.O. Box 811951
Amman
Jordan
Tel: 962 6 563 2204
Tel: 962 6 563 2000
Fax: 962 6 510 5916
Fax: 962 6 563 1020
E-mail: Heyam.Wahbeh@jfda.jo

Issues authorizations for import and export of narcotic drugs, psychotropic substances and precursor chemicals.

Article 12

Department of Drug and Forgery
Ministry of Interior
P.O. Box 100
Amman
Jordan
Tel: 962 6 5702811
Tel: 962 6 5691141
Fax: 962 6 5606908

Law enforcement.

Kazakhstan — Kazajstán

Articles 18, 16

Committee to combat drug trafficking and control the licit
    trade in drugs
Ministry of Interior
1, Tauelsizdik Street
Astana 0100000
Kazakhstan
Tel: 7 7172 714 588
Fax: 7 7172 714 588

Article 12

Deputy Minister, Ministry of Interior
Committee for the Fight Against Drug Abuse
    and Illicit Drug Trafficking
Astana
Kazakhstan
Tel: 7 317 2 714 112
Fax: 7 317 2 714 609
Fax: 7 317 2 714 682
Fax: 7 317 2 372 426
E-mail: un@kazakhstan.at

Kenya

Articles 18, 16

The Registrar, Pharmacy and Poisons Board
Ministry of Health
P.O. Box 30016
Nairobi
Kenya
Tel: 254 20 717077
Fax: 254 20 713750

Article 12(*)

The Registrar
Pharmacy and Poisons Board
P.O. Box 27663-00506
Nairobi
Kenya
Tel: 254 733 88 44 11
Tel: 254 720 608 811
Tel: 254 020 356 2107
Fax: 254 271 3409
Fax: 254 271 3431
E-mail: info@pharmacyboardkenya.org
E-mail: chiefpharm@health.go.ke

Kiribati

Articles 18, 16

Ministry of Health, Family Planning and Social
  Welfare
P.O. Box 268
Bikenibeu
Tarawa
Kiribati
Tel: 686 28100
Fax: 686 28152

Article 12(*)

Chief of Curative and Health Services
Ministry of Health, Family Planning and Social Welfare
P.O. Box 268
Bikenibeu
Tarawa
Kiribati
Tel: 686 28081 227
Tel: 686 28100
Fax: 686 28152

Kuwait - Koweït

Articles 18, 16

Ministry of Health
P.O. Box 4575
Safat 13046
Kuwait
Tel: 965 483 9045
Fax: 965 483 9045

Article 12(*)

The Under-Secretary, Ministry of Health
P.O. Box No 4575
13046 Safat
Kuwait
Tel: 965 486 5415
Tel: 965 486 0351
Fax: 965 486 5414

For policy matters.

Article 12(*)

Narcotic and Psychotropic
Drugs Licensing Control
Drug and Food Control Affairs
Ministry of Health
P.O. Box 4575
Safat 13046
Kuwait
Tel: 965 246 20221
Fax: 965 248 39045

For technical matters.

Kyrgyzstan — Kirghizistan — Kirguistán

Articles 18, 16, 12(*)

State Drug Control Service under the Government of the
Kyrgyz Republic
Ul. Toktogula 80
720021 Bishkek
The Kyrgyz Republic
Tel: 996 312 662217
Tel: 996 312 622263
Fax: 996 312 625143
E-mail: unn@gskn.kg
E-mail: pochta@gskn.kg

Lao People's Democratic Republic — République démocratique populaire Lao — República Democrática Popular Lao

Articles 18, 16

Ministry of Health
Food and Drug Department
Simuang Road
Vientiane Capital
Lao People's Democratic Republic
Tel: 856 21 214014
Tel: 856 21 214013
Fax: 856 21 214015
E-mail: drug@laotel.com
E-mail: cosmetic_laos@yahoo.com

Article 12(*)

Director General
Food and Drug Department
Ministry of Health
Simouang Road
Vientiane
Lao People's Democratic Republic
Tel: 856 21 214013-14
Fax: 856 21 214015
E-mail: lao_precurs456@yahoo.com.au

Latvia — Lettonie — Letonia

Articles 18, 16

State Agency of Medicines
15 Jersikas str.
1003 Riga
Latvia
Tel: 371 6 707 8424
Fax: 371 6 707 8428
E-mail: info@zva.gov.lv

Article 12

As regards legislation and coordination of administrative cooperation, please refer to entry of the European Union.

Head
Department of Information on Medicines Distribution
State Agency of Medicines
Ministry of Health
Jersikas Street 15
1003 Riga
Latvia
Tel: 371 6 707 8444
Tel: 371 6 707 8436
Fax: 371 6 707 8428
E-mail: Elma.Gailite@zva.gov.lv

Issuing licenses, import/export authorizations for the narcotic and psychotropic substances and precursors as well as for timely submission of reports, and requests for quota calculation for narcotics and psychotropic substances and precursors.

Lebanon — Liban — Líbano

Articles 18, 16, 12

Ministère de la santé publique
Département de la pharmacie
Service des stupéfiants
Quartier du musée
Beyrouth
Liban
Tel: 961 1 615745
Fax: 961 1 615730
E-mail: dep-narcotic@public-health.gov.lb

Lesotho

Articles 18, 16

Director of Pharmaceuticals
Ministry of Health
P.O. Box 514
Maseru 100
Lesotho
Tel: 266 2231 4404
Fax: 266 2231 0279

Article 12

Director of Pharmaceuticals
Ministry of Health
P.O. Box 514
Maseru 100
Lesotho
Tel: 266 2222 6000
Tel: 266 2222 6291
Fax: 266 2231 0004

Import/export authorization and statistical returns.

Article 12

Customs and Excise Department
P.O. Box 891
Maseru 100
Lesotho
Tel: 266 2231 3796
Fax: 266 2231 0390

Enforcement and border control.

Article 12

Department of Police
P.O. Box 13
Maseru 100
Lesotho
Tel: 266 2231 7262
Fax: 266 2231 0045

Enforcement, control.

Liberia — Libéria

(Article not specified)

Chief Pharmacist
Ministry of Health and Social Welfare
P.O. Box 10-9009
1000, Monrovia 10
Liberia
Tel: 231 226 317
Fax: 231 226 317

Libya — Libye — Libia

Articles 18, 16

Secretariat of Health and Environment
Pharmacy and Medical Equipment Department
El Sabaa Road
Tripoli - Elfornaj
Libyan Arab Jamahiriya
Tel: 218 21 463 0993
Fax: 218 21 463 0990

Article 12

Head
Medicines and Narcotics Sector
Pharmacy and Medical Devices Department
Ministry of Health
Elfornaj, El Sabaa Road
Tripoli
Libya
Tel: 218 21 463 0993
Fax: 218 21 463 1342
E-mail: fnrrama@yahoo.com

Liechtenstein

Articles 18, 16

Swissmedic
Swiss Agency for Therapeutic Products
Hallerstrasse 7
3000 Bern
Switzerland
Tel: 41 31 322 0211
Fax: 41 31 322 0212

Lithuania — Lituanie — Lituania

Articles 18, 12

State Medicines Control Agency under the
  Ministry of Health of the Republic of Lithuania
Zirmunu Street 139A
LT-09120 Vilnius
Lithuania
Tel: 370 5 261 6549
Tel: 370 5 261 6549
E-mail: vvkt@vvkt.lt

Article 16

Drug, Tobacco and Alcohol Control Department
St. Stepono Str. 27
Vilnius
Lithuania
Tel: 370 7066 8065
Tel: 370 7066 8060
Fax: 370 7066 8095
E-mail: julita.siuipiene@ntakd.lt
E-mail: ntakd@ntakd.lt

Article 12

As regards legislation and coordination of administrative cooperation, please refer to entry of the European Union.

Director
Drug, Tobacco and Alcohol control Department (NTAKD)
Ministry of Health
Šv. Stepono str. 27
Vilnius
Lithuania
Tel: 370 7066 8065
Tel: 370 7066 8060
Fax: 370 7066 8095
E-mail: rima.maciuniene@ntakd.lt
E-mail: ntakd@ntakd.lt

Luxembourg — Luxemburgo

Articles 18, 16

Direction de la santé
Division de la pharmacie et des médicaments
Villa Louvigny
Allée Marconi
2120 Luxembourg
Tel: 352 247 85593
Fax: 352 247 95615
E-mail: jacqueline.genoux-hames@ms.etat.lu

Article 12

As regards legislation and coordination of administrative cooperation, please refer to entry of the European Union.

Director, Direction de la santé
Division de la pharmacie et des médicaments
Villa Louvigny
Allée Marconi
Luxembourg
Tel: 352 247 85593
Tel: 352 247 85590
Fax: 352 247 95615
E-mail: jacqueline.genoux-hames@ms.etat.lu

Register of operators, issuing export authorizations and other permits.

Article 12

As regards legislation and coordination of administrative cooperation, please refer to entry of the European Union.

Administration des Douanes et Accises
Division Anti-Drogues et Produits Sensibles
Cellule Précurseurs Chimiques
B.P. 1605
L-1016 Luxembourg
Tel: 352 2818 2281
Fax: 352 2828 9230
E-mail: Michelle.Wolff@do.etat.lu

Control and investigation.

Macao Special Administrative Region (SAR) of China – Région administrative spéciale (RAS)de Macao (Chine) – Región Administrativa Especial (RAE) de Macao de China

Articles 18, 16

Department of Pharmaceutical Affairs, Health Bureau
Av. Sidónio Pais No. 51 – 2°andar China Plaza
Macao SAR of China
Tel: 853 598 3525
Fax: 853 2852 4016
E-mail: daf@ssm.gov.mo

Article 12

Foreign Trade Division
Foreign Trade Management Department
Macao Economic Services
Rua Dr. Pedro Jose Lobo, 1-3
Luso International Bank Building, 2/F
Maca SAR of China
Tel: 853 8597 2637
Fax: 853 2871 5633
E-mail: dgce@economia.gov.mo

Article 12

Control and issue of import/export authorizations
Head
Narcotics Division
Judiciary Police
Avenida Da Amizade No. 823
Macao SAR of China
Tel: 853 2835 6100
Tel: 853 2883 3777
Fax: 853 2883 9496
E-mail: Piquete.sede@pj.gov.mo
E-mail: dicte@pj.gov.mo

Madagascar

Articles 18, 16

Direction des pharmacies, du laboratoire et de la
   médecine traditionnelle
B.P. 22 bis
Antananarivo 101
Madagascar
Tel: 261 33 11 219 88
Tel: 261 20 22 323 00
E-mail: minsandpl@wanadoo.mg

Article 12

Directeur de la Pharmacie, des Laboratoires et de la
   Médecine Traditionnelle
Ministére de la Santé Publique
B.P. 22 bis Tsaralalàna
Antananarivo 101
Madagascar
Tel: 261 32 48 960 68
Tel: 261 20 22 200 97
Fax: 261 20 22 642 28
E-mail: dplmt@sante.gov.mg

Malawi

Articles 18, 16

Secretary for Health
Ministry of Health and Population
P.O. Box 30377
Lilongwe 3
Malawi
Tel: 265 783 044

Article 12

The Registrar
Pharmacy, Medicines and Poisons Board (PMPB)
P.O. Box 30241
Lilongwe 3
Malawi
Tel: 265 1 755165
Fax: 265 1 755204
E-mail: pmpb@broadbandmw.com
E-mail: admin@pmpb.malawi.net.com

Malaysia — Malaisie — Malasia

Articles 18, 16

Pharmaceutical Services Division
Ministry of Health
Lot 36
Jalan Universiti
46350 Petaling Jaya
Selangor Darul Ehsan
Malaysia
Tel: 60 3 7841 3200
Fax: 60 3 7968 2222
E-mail: eisah@moh.gov.my

Malaysia — Malaisie — Malasia
(continued — suite — continuación)

Article 12

Pharmaceutical Services Division
Ministry of Health Malaysia
Lot 36, Jalan Universiti
46350 Petaling Jaya, Selangor
Malaysia
Tel: 60 3 7968 3200
Fax: 60 3 7968 2251
Fax: 60 3 7968 2222
E-mail: tankeel@moh.gov.my
E-mail: suliati@moh.gov.my
E-mail: latifahi@moh.gov.my

Licenses importers and distributors of: acetic anhydride, ephedrine, ergometrine, ergotamine, ethyl ether, hydrochloric acid, sulphuric acid, pseudoephedrine. Issues approval permit for import and export of acetic anhydride, ephedrine and pseudoephedrine. Receiving pre-export notifications. Replies to enquiries. Cooperates with customs and police to carry out controlled delivery.

Maldives — Maldivas

Articles 18, 16

Ministry of Health
Ameenee Magu
Malé
Maldives
Tel: 960 328 887
Fax: 960 328 889

Article 12

Ministry of Foreign Affairs
Boduthakurufaanu Magu, Post code: 26077
Malé
Maldives
Tel: 960 323 400
Fax: 960 323 841
E-mail: der@foreign.gov.mv

Mali — Malí

Articles 18, 16

Ministère de la santé
Direction de la pharmacie et du médicament
B.P. E5202, Rue 560, limite centre commercial-Darsalam
Bamako
Mali
Tel: 223 222 6570
Fax: 223 223 2463
E-mail: mmaiga@dirpharma.org

Article 16

Ministère de la santé
Direction de la pharmacie et du médicament
B.P. E5202, Rue 560, limite centre commercial-Darsalam
Bamako
Mali
Tel: 223 222 6570
Fax: 223 223 2324
Fax: 223 223 2463
E-mail: pharmali@datatech.toolnet.org

Article 12(*)

Direction de la pharmacie et du médicament
B.P. E 5202, Rue 560, limite centre commercial,
    Darsalam
Bamako
Mali
Tel: 223 222 6570
Fax: 223 223 2463
E-mail: mmaiga@dirpharma.org

Malta — Malte

Articles 18, 16, 12

Superintendence of Public Health
SLH - OPD (Level 1),
St. Luke's Square, G'Mangia
Malta
Tel: 356 2595 3300
Fax: 356 2595 3304
E-mail: victor.p.pace@gov.mt

Marshall Islands — Îles Marshall — Islas Marshall

Articles 18, 16

Ministry of Health Services
P.O. Box 16
Majuro 96960
Marshall Islands
Tel: 692 625 3355
Fax: 692 625 4543
E-mail: jusmoshe@ntamar.net

Martinique - Martinica

Articles 18, 16

Direction régionale des affaires sanitaires et sociales
Inspection des pharmacies
B.P. 656
97263 Fort-de-France
Martinique
Tel: 596 570 170

Article 12

Mission nationale de Contrôle des Précurseurs
  Chimiques (MNCPC)
Direction Générale des Enterprises (DGE)
67 rue Barbès 94201 Ivry sur Seine Cedex
France
Tel: 33 1 7984 3169
Fax: 33 1 7984 3637
E-mail: mncpc@finances.gouv.fr

Mauritania — Mauritanie

Articles 18, 16

Ministère de la santé et des affaires sociales
Direction des pharmacies
B.P. 169
Nouakchott
Mauritanie
Tel: 222 2 52052
Fax: 222 2 52268

Mauritius — Maurice — Mauricio

Articles 18, 16

Senior Chief Executive, Ministry of Health and Quality of
  Life
Directorate of Pharmacy
Emmanuel Anquetil Building, 5th floor
Port-Louis
Mauritius
Tel: 230 201 1334
Fax: 230 201 3891
E-mail: chpheist@intnet.mu

Article 12

Permanent Secretary
Ministry of Health
Emmanuel Anquetil Building, 5th floor
Port-Louis
Mauritius
Tel: 230 201 1334
Tel: 230 201 1912
Fax: 230 208 7222
Fax: 230 208 0376

Issuing import/export authorization.

Article 12

Comptroller of Customs
Customs and Excise Department
IKS Building
Port-Louis
Mauritius
Tel: 230 240 9090
Fax: 230 240 0434

Mexico — Mexique — México

Articles 18, 16, 12

Centro Nacional de Planeación, Análisis e
  Información para el Combate a la Delincuencia
  (CENAPI)
Agencia de Investigación
Procuraduría General de la República (PGR)
Xóchitil No. 30
Col. Pueblo San Pablo Tepetlapa
Delegación Coyoacán
C.P. 04640 México, D.F
México
Tel: 52 55-5169 6557
Tel: 52 55 5169 6501
Fax: 52 55 5169 6672
E-mail: quimicos@pgr.gob.mx
E-mail: veronica.espana@pgr.gob.mx
E-mail: cenapi.staff@pgr.gob.mx

Law enforcement and investigation. General coordination
of information sharing between Mexican and foreign
authorities. Replies to inquiries and pre-export
notifications for substances in Table II of the 1988
Convention.

Article 12

Director Ejecutivo
Regulación de Estupefacientes,
  Psicotropicos y Sustancias Quimicas
Comisión Federal para la Proteccion
  contra Riesgos Sanitarios (COFEPRIS)
Oklahoma No. 14, Piso 2, Colonia Nápoles
Delegación Benito Juárez
C.P. 03810, México, D.F.
Tel: 52 555080 5200 ext1041/1045
Fax: 52 55 5511 1365
E-mail: renava@cofepris.gob.mx

Micronesia (Federated States of) – Micronésie (États fédérés de) – Micronesia (Estados Federados de)

Articles 18, 16

Secretary, Department of Health Services
P.O. Box PS 70
Palikir, Pohnpei FM 96941
Micronesia (Federated States of)
Tel: 691 320 2872
Tel: 691 320 2619
Tel: 691 320 2643
Fax: 691 320 5263

Article 12

Secretary, Department of Health and Social Affairs
Division of Health Services
P.O. Box PS 70
Palikir, Pohnpei FM 96941
Micronesia (Federated States of)
Tel: 691 320 2643
Tel: 691 320 2619
Tel: 691 320 2872
Fax: 691 320 5263
E-mail: health@fsmhealth.fm

Monaco — Mónaco

Articles 18, 16

Police de Monaco
Section de la coopération internationale
9 rue Suffren Raymond
98000 Monaco
Monaco
Tel: 377 9315 3323
Fax: 377 9350 8746
E-mail: ybarelli@gouv.mc

Article 12

Direction de l'action sanitaire et sociale
13, rue Émile de Loth
98000 Monaco
Monaco
Tel: 377 98 98 83 10
Fax: 377 98 98 81 59

Mongolia — Mongolie

Article 18

Ministry of Health
Government Building 8
Olympic Street 2
Ulaanbaatar 210648
Mongolia
Tel: 976 11 263 913
Fax: 976 11 320 916
E-mail: admin@moh.mn

Article 16

General Police Department
Sambuu Street 18
Chingeltei district
Ulaanbaatar 211238
Mongolia
Tel: 976 11 325 507
Fax: 976 11 322 057
E-mail: gpdint@mongol.net

Montenegro — Monténégro

Articles 18, 16

Ministry of Health, Labour and Social Welfare
Rimski Trg 46
Podgorica
Montenegro
Tel: 382 20 242 342
Fax: 382 20 242 762
E-mail: mzdravlja@mn.yu

Article 12

Agency for Medicines and Medical Devices
Ul.II Cmogorskog Bataljona b.b.
81 000 Podgorica
Montenegro
Tel: 382 20 310 280
Fax: 382 20 310 280
E-mail: jasmina.krlic@calims.me

Issuing licenses for import/export of narcotic drugs, psychotropic substances and precursors

Montserrat - Montserrat - Montserrat

Article 12(*)

Director, Health Services
Health Department
Ministry of Education, Health & Community Services
P.O. Box 24
Plymouth
Montserrat
Tel: 1 664 491 2552
Tel: 1 664 491 2880
Fax: 1 664 491 3131
Fax: 1 664 491 4533

Article

Attorney-General
Attorney-General's Office
P.O. Box 129
Plymouth
Montserrat
Tel: 1 664 491 4686
Tel: 1 664 491 5180
Fax: 1 664 491 4687

Article

Comptroller of Customs
Plymouth
Montserrat
Tel: 1 664 491 6909

Morocco — Maroc — Marruecos

Articles 18, 16

Direction du médicament et de la pharmacie
Service des Stupéfiants
Ministère de la Santé
B.P. 6206
Rue Lamfaddal Charkaoui
Rabat
Maroc
Tel: 212 5 37 77 06 45
Tel: 212 5 37 68 22 89
Fax: 212 5 37 68 19 31
E-mail: n_mouhssine@hotmail.com

Article 12

Le Secrétaire général
Ministère de la Santé
Direction du Médicament et de la Pharmacie
Service des Stupéfiants
B.P. 6206
Rabat
Maroc
Tel: 212 5 37 77 28 33
Tel: 212 5 37 77 06 45
Fax: 212 5 37 68 19 31
Fax: 212 5 37 77 16 41

Approve the pharmaceutical use of precursor chemicals.

Article 12

Direction de la Politique des Échanges Commerciaux
Ministère du Commerce Extérieur
Division de la Réglementation et
  de la Facilitation Commerciale
63, Avenue Moulay Youssef
Rabat
Morocco
Tel: 212 5 37 70 18 46
Fax: 212 5 37 72 71 50
E-mail: elalaoui@mce.gov.ma
E-mail: boutarbouch@mce.gov.ma
E-mail: maafiri@mce.gov.ma

Approve the industrial use of precursor chemicals.

Mozambique

Articles 18, 16

Pharmaceutical Department
Ministry of Health
Av. Salvador Allende/Agostinho Neto
Maputo
Mozambique
Tel: 258 21 303 447
Fax: 258 21 326 547

Myanmar

Articles 18, 16

Supervisory Committee for Controlled Precursor
  Chemicals
Building No. 8,
Headquarters of Myanmar Police Force
Nay Pyi Taw
Myanmar
Tel: 95 67 412033
Fax: 95 67 412033

Article 12

Head of Department
Central Committee for Drug Abuse Control (CCDAC)
Myanmar Police Force Headquarters
Building No. 8
Ministry of Home Affairs
Nay Pyi Taw
Myanmar
Tel: 95 9 6741 2915
Fax: 95 6741 2033
Fax: 95 6741 2544
Fax: 95 9 6741 2136
E-mail: ccdac.ir199@gmail.com
E-mail: ccdac.pm@gmail.com

Namibia — Namibie

Articles 18, 16

Ministry of Health and Social Services
Private Bag 13198
Windhoek
Namibia
Tel: 264 61 203 9111
Fax: 264 61 231 784

Article 12

Permanent Secretary, Medicines Control Council
Ministry of Health and Social Services
P.B. 13366
Windhoek
Namibia
Tel: 264 61 203 2861
Fax: 264 61 221 332
Fax: 264 61 227 607

Administers legislation. No system to monitor chemicals is yet in place.

Article 12

Inspector-General, Namibian Police
Drug Enforcement Unit
P.B. 12024, Aussamplatz
Windhoek
Namibia
Tel: 264 61 230 410
Tel: 264 61 231 388
Fax: 264 61 220 621

Law enforcement.

Nauru

Article

The Director of Health and Medical Services
Department of Health
Nauru

Nepal — Népal

Articles 18, 16

Joint Secretary
Chief Narcotics Control Officers
Planning and Special Service Division
Ministry of Home Affairs
Singh Durbar
Kathmandu
Nepal
Tel: 977 9841 555 675 (mobile)
Tel: 977 1 421 1241
Fax: 977 1 421 1283
E-mail: koirala_shankarp@yahoo.com

Article 12

Under Secretary, Narcotic Control Section
Ministry of Home Affairs
Singh Durbar
Kathmandu
Nepal
Tel: 977 9741 072 055 (mobile)
Tel: 977 1 421 1237
Fax: 977 1 421 1283
E-mail: bldvgautam@gmail.com

Issuance of import licenses for substances included in Table I of the 1988 Convention.

Article 12(*)

Chief Narcotic Drug Control Law Enforcement Division (NDCLEU)
New Baneshower
Kathmandu
Nepal
Tel: 977 9851 000983 (mobile)
Tel: 977 1 478 1708
Fax: 977 1 478 1578
E-mail: yadavadhikari@hotmail.com

Enforcement authority. Monitoring, inspection of diversion of precursors.

Article 12(*)

Department of Drug Administration (DDA)
Ministry of Health and Population
Madan Bhandari Path — 4
Bijuli Bazzar
New Banewshor
Kathmandu
Nepal
Tel: 977 1 478 0227
Tel: 977 1 478 0432
Fax: 977 1 478 0572
E-mail: dda@healthnet.org.np

Netherlands — Pays-Bas — Países Bajos

Articles 18, 16

CIBG/Health Care Inspectorate
Farmatec / RK4
P.O. Box 16114
2500 BC The Hague
The Netherlands
Tel: 31 70 340 6278
E-mail: w.best@igz.nl

Article 12

As regards legislation and coordination of administrative cooperation, please refer to entry of the European Union.

Fiscal Intelligence and Investigation Service (FIOD)
Central Precursor Unit / National Focal Point
Waagstraat 1, 5611 KZ Eindhoven
Postbus 90051, 5600 PC Eindhoven
The Netherlands
Tel: 31 6 1860 20 08 (mobile)
Tel: 31 40 265 65 00
Fax: 31 40 265 6599
E-mail: ham.hendriks@belastingdienst.nl

Investigation.

Article 12
As regards legislation and coordination of administrative cooperation, please refer to entry of the European Union.

Customs and Excise Service
Central Service for Imports and Exports
P. O. Box 3003
NL-9700 RD Groningen
Netherlands
Tel: 31 88 151 21 22
Fax: 31 88 151 31 82
E-mail: drn-cdiu.groningen@belastingdienst.nl

Licensing, pre-export notifications and registration.

New Caledonia – Nouvelle-Calédonie – Nueva Caledonia

Articles 18, 16

Inspection de la pharmacie
Direction des affaires sanitaires et sociales
5, rue du général Gallieni
B.P. N4
98851 Nouméa Cedex
Nouvelle-Calédonie
Tel: 687 243 717
Fax: 687 243 733

Article 12

Mission nationale de Contrôle des Précurseurs
   Chimiques (MNCPC)
Direction Générale des Enterprises (DGE)
67 rue Barbès 94201 Ivry sur Seine Cedex
France
Tel: 33 1 7984 3169
Fax: 33 1 7984 3637
E-mail: mncpc@finances.gouv.fr

New Zealand — Nouvelle-Zélande — Nueva Zelandia

Articles 18, 16

The Director-General of Health
Licensing Authority
Medicines Control, Provider Regulation
Clinical Leadership, Protection and Regulation(CLPR)
Ministry of Health
PO Box 5013
Wellington 6145
New Zealand
Tel: 64 4 496 2018
Fax: 64 4 496 2229
E-mail: medicinescontrol@moh.govt.nz

Article 12

National Drug Intelligence Bureau
Police National HQ
P.O. Box 3017
180 Molesworth Street
Wellington
New Zealand
Tel: 64 4 474 9499
Tel: 64 4 474 8859
Fax: 64 4 473 7634
E-mail: ndib@police.govt.nz

Nicaragua

Articles 18, 16

Ministerio de Salud
Contiguo a la Colonia Primero de Mayo
Managua
Nicaragua
Tel: 505 289 4401
Fax: 505 289 4401
E-mail: div-far@minsa.gob.ni

Article 12(*)

Directora, División de Farmacia
Ministerio de Salud
"Dra Concepción Palacios"
Managua
Nicaragua
Tel: 505 289 7601
Fax: 505 289 4401
E-mail: farmaciadir@minsa.gob.ni
E-mail: controldrogas@minsa.gob.nl
E-mail: areadrogas@minsa.gob.ni

Niger — Níger

Articles 18, 16

Directeur de la pharmacie et des laboratoires
Ministère de la santé publique
B.P. 623
Niamey
Níger
Tel: 227 20 722 782
Fax: 227 20 723 025

Article 12

Directeur de la pharmacie et des laboratoires
Ministère de la santé publique
B.P. 623
Niamey
Níger
Tel: 227 20 722 782
Fax: 227 20 733 570

Nigeria — Nigéria

Articles 18, 16

National Agency for Food and Drugs Administration and
   Control (NAFDAC)
Plot 2032 Olusegun Obasanjo Way
Wuse 7
Abuja
Nigeria
Tel: 234 9 671 8008
E-mail: nafdac@nafdac.gov.ng

Article 12

Director-General, National Agency for Food and Drugs
Administration and Control (NAFDAC)
Plot 2032, Olusegun Obasanjo Way, Wuse, Zone 7
Abuja
Nigeria
Tel: 234 80 331 55380
Tel: 234 1 474 4549
Tel: 234 1 473 0875
Fax: 234 1 269 0307
E-mail: yusufu.h@nafdac.gov.ng
E-mail: ebigbeyi.m@nafdac.gov.ng
E-mail: ncs@nafdac.gov.ng

Authorization of imports of substances in Tables I and II
of the 1988 Convention.

Norfolk Island – Île Norfolk – Isla Norfolk

Articles 18, 16

Drug Control Section, Office of Scientific Evaluation
Therapeutic Goods Administration
Department of Health
P.O. Box 100
Woden ACT 2606
Australia
Tel: 61 2 6232 8740
Fax: 61 2 6203 1740
E-mail: dcs@tga.gov.au

Article 12

Director
Drug Control Section, Office of Scientific Evaluation
Therapeutic Goods Administration
Department of Health
PO Box 100
Woden ACT 2606, Australia
Tel: 61 2 6232 8740
Fax: 61 2 6203 1740
E-mail: dcs@tga.gov.au
Web: www.tga.gov.au

Norway — Norvège — Noruega

Articles 18, 16

Norwegian Medicines Agency (Statens legemiddelverk)
P.O.Box 63, Kalbakken
0901 Oslo
Norway
Tel: 47 22 89 77 00
Fax: 47 22 89 77 99
E-mail: post@noma.no

Article 12

Norwegian Medicines Agency
Statens legemiddelverk)
P.O. Box 63, Kalbakken
0901 Oslo
Norway
Tel: 47 22 89 77 00
Fax: 47 22 89 77 99
E-mail: post@noma.no

Licensing,   registration,   pre-export   notifications,
import/export authorizations.

Article 12

Directorate of Customs and Excise
Toll – og avgiftsdirektoratet
P.O. Box 8122 Dep.
0032 Oslo
Norway
Tel: 47 22 86 03 00
Fax: 47 22 86 08 00
E-mail: desken@toll.no

Article 12

Border control, control of import and export
National Criminal Investigation Service (Kripos)
P.O. Box 8163 Dep.
0034 Oslo
Norway
Tel: 47 23 20 8000
Fax: 47 23 20 8880
E-mail: kripos@politiet.no

Investigation, seizure statistics.

Oman — Omán

Articles 18, 16

Director-General
Pharmaceutical Affairs and Drug Control
Ministry of Health
P.O. Box 393
Muscat, P.C. 100
Oman
Tel: 968 246 00016
Tel: 968 246 94744
Fax: 968 246 92107
Fax: 968 246 02287

Article 12

The Director-General of Criminal Inquiries and
   Investigation
Directorate of Drug Enforcement
Royal Oman Police
P.O. Box 446
Muscat, P.C. 113
Oman
Tel: 968 2456 9311
Fax: 968 2457 1040
E-mail: dgdsc@rop.gov.om

Seizure statistics.

Article 12

Directorate General of Environmental Affairs, Chemicals
   Department
Ministry of Regional Municipalities, Environment and
   Water Resources
P.O. Box 323, Postal Code 113
Muscat
Oman
Tel: 968 2440 4776
Tel: 968 2440 4774
Fax: 968 2440 4796
E-mail: Chemical_dept@meca.gov.om

Licensing.

Pakistan — Pakistán

Articles 18, 16

Secretary, Ministry of Narcotics Control, Drug Control
   Administration, Cabinet Division
Block C, 3rd Floor, Pak Sectt, IBD
Islamabad
Pakistan
Tel: 92 51 920 2566
Fax: 92 51 920 5216
E-mail: Abdullah.ak@gmail.com

Article 12

Director-General, Anti-Narcotics Force
National Park Road
Rawalpindi
Pakistan
Tel: 92 51 9260535
Fax: 92 51 9261896
E-mail: anf@anf.gov.pk

Central coordinating authority to prevent diversion of
chemicals and substances, and law enforcement.

Article 12

The Secretary
Ministry of Narcotics Control
House No. 30, Street 48
Sector F-8/4
Islamabad
Pakistan
Tel: 92 51 926 0535
Fax: 92 51 926 1896
E-mail: secretary@narcon.gov.pk

Policy formulation for drug control.

Pakistan — Pakistán

(continued — suite — continuación)

Article 12

Chief Executive Officer
Drug Regulatory Agency of Pakistan (DRAP)
Ministry of National Regulations and Services
C-Block Pak Secretariat
Islamabad
Pakistan

Control of substances in Table I of the 1988 Convention. In particular, verification of the legitimacy of ephedrine and pseudoephedrine.

Panama — Panamá

Articles 18, 16

Dirección Nacional de Farmacia y Drogas
Ministerio de Salud
06812 Zona Postal 0816
Panamá
Panamá
Tel: 507 512 9162
Tel: 507 512 9167
Fax: 507 212 9196
E-mail: narcoticos@minsa.gob.pa

Article 12(*)

Secretaria Ejecutiva
Comisión Nacional para el Estudio y la Prevención de los Delitos Relacionados con Drogas (CONAPRED)
Edificio Aveso, Primer Piso
Via España
Panamá
Panamá
Tel: 507 505 3252
Fax: 507 505 3254
E-mail: ucq.conapred@procuraduria.gob.pa
E-mail: controldequimicos@gmail.com

Papua New Guinea — Papouasie-Nouvelle-Guinée — Papua Nueva Guinea

Article 18

Director General, National Narcotics Bureau
P.O. Box 3880
Boroko, NCD
Port Moresby
Papua New Guinea
Tel: 675 325 0910
Fax: 675 325 8842

Article 16

Secretary, Department of Health
P.O. Box 807
Waigani, NCD
Port Moresby
Papua New Guinea
Tel: 675 301 3827
Fax: 675 323 9669

Article 12(*)

Director, National Narcotics Bureau
P.O. Box 3880, Boroko, NCD
Port Moresby
Papua New Guinea
Tel: 675 325 0691
Tel: 675 325 0910
Fax: 675 325 8842

Article 12(*)

Controller of Customs, Bureau of Customs and Excise
Ministry of Finance
Boroko, NCD
Port Moresby
Papua New Guinea

Article 12(*)

Secretary, Department of Health
P.O. Box 807 Waigani, Boroko, NCD
Port Moresby
Papua New Guinea
Tel: 675 301 3886
Fax: 675 323 1631

Paraguay

Articles 18, 16

Ministerio de Salud Pública y Bienestar Social
Brasil 783, esq. Fulgelcio R. Moreno
Asunción
Paraguay
Tel: 595 21 204 601
Fax: 595 21 204 770

Article 12

Dirección Nacional de Vigilancia Sanitaria
Ministerio de Salud Pública y Bienestar Social (MSP y BS)
Pasaje San Carlos 916 entre Fulgencio R. Moreno y Manuel Dominguez
Asunción
Paraguay
Tel: 595 21 204 770
Tel: 595 21 214 934
Fax: 595 21 204 715
E-mail: dnvs@mspbs.gov.py

Responsible for all precursors.

Article 12

Secretaría Nacional Antidrogas (SENAD)
Direccioón de Registro y Control de la SENAD
Avenida Fernando de la Mora 2998
Asunción
Paraguay
Tel: 595 21 202 679
Fax: 595 21 554 585
Fax: 595 21 554 584
E-mail: senadcooperacion@gmail.com
E-mail: darimartin.a@gmail.com
E-mail: derfisenad@gmail.com

Peru — Pérou — Perú

Article 18

Dirección General de Medicamentos Insumos y Drogas
  (DIGEMID)
Ministerio de Salud
Av. Parque de las Leyendas Cdra. 1
Lote 2, Mz. 1-3, Urb. Pando – San Miguel
Lima 32
Perú
Tel: 511 631 4300 ext. 6007
Fax: 511 453 2061
E-mail: kclavijo@digemid.minsa.gob.pe
E-mail: dg@digemid.minsa.gob.pe

Article 16

Dirección de Insumos Químicos y Productos
  Fiscalizados
Ministerio de la Producción
Calle Uno Oeste No. 060, Urb. Corpac
San Isidro
Lima 27
Peru
Tel: 51 1 616 2206
Fax: 51 1 224 3141
E-mail: insuqui@produce.gob.pe

Article 12

Director-General, Dirección General de Medicamentos,
  Insumos y Drogas (DIGEMID)
Ministerio de Salud
Av. Parque las Leyendas Cdra. 1
Lote 2, Mz.1-3, Urb. Pando –San Miguel – Lima 32
Perú
Tel: 51 1 6314300 Anexo 6007
Fax: 51 1 4522061
E-mail: kclavijo@digemid.minsa.gob.pe
E-mail: dg@digemid.minsa.gob.pe

Issues import certificates for substances used in manufacture of pharmaceutical preparations. Receives, in particular, preexport notifications for ephedrine, ergometrine, ergotamine, lysergic acid, norephedrine and pseudoephedrine.

Article 12

Directora
Dirección de insumos Químicos y Productos Fiscalizados
Ministerio de Producción (PRODUCE)
Calle Uno s/n, Urb. Córpac
San Isidro
Lima 27
Perú
Tel: 51 1 616 2206
Fax: 51 1 224 3141
E-mail: insuqui@produce.gob.pe

Control of chemical substances through import/export certificates which specifically show the entry and exit of the substances in the country. Furthermore, the exporters should ask for the corresponding authorization for each transaction. Receives, in particular, pre-export notifications for acetic anhydride, acetone, ethyl ether, hydrochloric acid, methyl ethyl ketone, potassium permanganate, sulphuric acid and toluene.

Article 12

Jefe, División de Investigación y Control de Insumos
  Químicos – DICQ-DINANDRO-PNP
Policia Nacional del Perú
Dirección Ejecutiva Antidrogas
Jr. Restauración Nro. 600- Breña
Lima
Perú
Tel: 51 1 424 9440
E-mail: coord_diviciq@hotmail.com

Control of manufacture, trade, imports/exports, transport and use of chemical substances under control.

Article 12

Presidente Ejecutivo
Comisión Nacional para el Desarrollo y Vida sin Drogas
  (DEVIDA)
Av. Benavides 2199 - B
Lima 18
Perú
Tel: 51 1 207 4800 ext, 1222
Fax: 51 1 271 1140
E-mail: compromisoglobal@devida.gob.pe
E-mail: mschreiber@devida.gob.pe

Philippines — Filipinas

Articles 18, 16

Compliance Service, Philippine Drug Enforcement
  Agency
PDEA Bldg., NIA, Northside Rd., Brgy. Pinyahan,
Quezon City
Philippines
Tel: 63 2 920 8110
Fax: 63 2 920 8110
Fax: 63 2 927 2899
E-mail: pdea_cs@yahoo.com.ph

Philippines — Filipinas
(continued — suite — continuación)

Article 12

Compliance Service, Philippine Drug Enforcement
   Agency (PDEA)
Rm 213, PDEA Bldg.
National Government Center, Pinyahan
Quezon City
Philippines
Tel: 63 2 9279 702 197
Tel: 63 2 9279 702 198
Tel: 63 2 9279 702 115
Fax: 63 2 9208 110
E-mail: pdea_cs@yahoo.com.ph

Issuing licenses to operate, issuing import and export
authorizations for narcotic drugs and psychotropic
substances, and enforcing national controls over
precursors and essential chemicals, pursuant to article of
the 1988 Convention.

Article 12

Bureau of Customs
Port Area
Manila
Philippines
Tel: 63 915 863 3548

Checks arrival/departure for substances in Table I and/or
Table II, the port entry /exit if with legal documents -
import/export permits.

Pitcairn

Articles 18, 16

The Commissioner for Pitcairn Islands
Level 10, Reserve Bank Building
67 Customs Street
Private Box 105696
Auckland
New Zealand
Tel: 64 9 366 0186
Fax: 64 9 366 0187
E-mail: admin@pitcairn.gov.pn

Poland — Pologne — Polonia

Articles 18, 16

Main Pharmaceutical Inspectorate
12 Senatorska Str.
00-082 Warsaw
Poland
Tel: 48 22 831 2131
Fax: 48 22 441 0702
Fax: 48 22 831 0244
E-mail: gif@gif.gov.pl

Article 12

As regards legislation and coordination of administrative
cooperation, please refer to entry of the European Union.

Chief Pharmaceutical Inspector
General Pharmaceutical Inspectorate
38/40 Dluga Street
00-238 Warsaw
Poland
Tel: 48 22 831 2131
Fax: 48 22 831 0244

Issues import/export authorizations. Control of Table I
substances.

Article 12

As regards legislation and coordination of administrative
cooperation, please refer to entry of the European Union.

Chief Sanitary Inspectorate
Department of Environmental Hygiene
38/40 Dluga Street
00-238 Warsaw
Poland
Tel: 48 22 635 4581
Fax: 48 22 635 6194
E-mail: inspektorat@gismz.gov.pl

Control of Table II substances.

Article 12

As regards legislation and coordination of administrative
cooperation, please refer to entry of the European Union.

National Police Headquarters
Central Narcotics Bureau, Komenda Glowna Policji
ul. Pulawska 148/150
02-624 Warsaw 12
Poland
Tel: 48 22 621 0251
Tel: 48 22 601 2883
Tel: 48 22 601 2384
Fax: 48 22 845 1183

Control and investigation.

Portugal

Articles 18, 16

INFARMED - National Authority of Medicines and Health
   Products, I.P.
Parque da Saúde de Lisboa
Avenida do Brasil, 53
1749-004 Lisboa
Portugal
Tel: 351 21 798 7268
Fax: 351 21 7987257
E-mail: infarmed@infarmed.pt

Article 12

As regards legislation and coordination of administrative cooperation, please refer to entry of the European Union.

SICAD - General Directorate on Addictive Behaviours
  And Dependencies
Avda República, 61, 8.º
1050-189 Lisboa
Portugal
Tel: 351 21 111 9100
E-mail: dri@sicad.min-saude.pt

To monitor application of relevant laws, and report in accordance with article 12, para. 12.

Article 12

As regards legislation and coordination of administrative cooperation, please refer to entry of the European Union.

AT - Tax and Customs Authority
Licensing Unit
Ministry of Finances
Rua da Alfândega nº 5 R/C
1149-006 Lisboa
Portugal
Tel: 351 21 881 3843
Fax: 351 21 881 3986
E-mail: Luisa.Vilhena.Nobre@at.gov.pt
E-mail: Antonio.Fernandes.Teixeira@at.gov.pt

Responsible for issuing import/export authorizations for substances listed in Tables I and II of the 1988 Convention. Licensing and registration and correspondent for Pre-Export Notification.

Article 12

As regards legislation and coordination of administrative cooperation, please refer to entry of the European Union.

DGAE - General Directorate of Economic Activities
Avenida Visconde Valmor No. 72
1069-041 Lisbon
Portugal
Tel: 351 21 791 9100
Fax: 351 21 796 5158
E-mail: dgae@dgae.pt

For monitoring the manufacture of substances listed in Tables I and II of the 1988 Convention

Article 12

As regards legislation and coordination of administrative cooperation, please refer to entry of the European Union.

AT - Tax and Customs Authority
Customs Antifraud Services
Intelligence Division
Ministry of Finances
Avª Duque de Ávila, nº 71, 2º andar
1000-139 LISBOA
Portugal
Tel: 351 21 358 4895
Fax: 351 21 358 4855
E-mail: dsafa-di@at.gov.pt

Customs Risk Management, including Control; to assess, in advance, the risk of any consignement arriving or leaving the European Union and to confiscate any illicit substance upon import, export or transit, as necessary.

Article 12

As regards legislation and coordination of administrative cooperation, please refer to entry of the European Union.

ASAE - Food and Economic Safety Authority
Ministry of Economy
Rua Rodrigo da Fonseca, nº. 73
1269-274 Lisboa, Portugal
Portugal
Tel: 351 21 798 3600
Fax: 351 21 798 3772
E-mail: correio.asae@asae.pt
E-mail: mcvitor@asae.pt
E-mail: arcarvalheiro@asae.pt
Web: www.asae.pt

Puerto Rico - Porto Rico

See information immediately under United States of America, **Articles 18, 16**

Qatar

Article 18

Drug Enforcement Department
P.O. Box 6797
Doha
Qatar
Tel: 974 4826 000
Fax: 974 4826 000

Article 16

Pharmacy and Drug Control Department
P.O. Box 1919
Doha
Qatar
Tel: 974 4423 985
Fax: 974 4425 399

Article 12

Director of Pharmacy and Drug Control Department
Supreme Council of Health
P.O. Box 42
Doha
Qatar
Tel: 974 4407 0799
Tel: 974 4407 0798
Fax: 974 4407 0808
E-mail: info@sch.gov.qa
Web: www.sch.gov.qa

Control of imports.

Republic of Korea — République de Corée — República de Corea

Articles 18, 16, 12

Director
Narcotics Policy Division
Ministry of Food and Drug Safety (MSDF)
Osong Health Technology
Administration Complex 187
Osongsaengmyeong-2ro, Osong-eup
Cheongwon-Gun, Chungbuk-do
363-700, Republic of Korea
Tel: 82 43 719 2801-2816
Fax: 82 43 719 2800
E-mail: narcotics@korea.kr

Article 12

Director, Narcotics Division
Supreme Public Prosecutors' Office
1730-1, Socho-Dong, Socho-Ku
Seoul
Republic of Korea
Tel: 82 2 535 0133
Fax: 82 2 3480 2718

Seizure statistics.

Republic of Moldova — République de Moldova— República de Moldova

Article 18

Ministry of Internal Affairs
Stefan cel Mare street, 75
2012 Chisinau
Moldova
Tel: 373 22 255 723
Fax: 373 22 226 321
E-mail: dciie@mai.gov.md

Article 16

Standing Committee on Narcotic Drug Control
8, Prunkul str.
Chisinau MD-2005
Republic of Moldova
Tel: 373 022 29 4091
Fax: 373 022 29 3596
E-mail: moprea@mail.ru

Article 12

President, Standing Committee on Narcotic Drugs
    Control
Ministry of Health
Pruncul str.8
MD-2005 Chisinau
Moldova
Tel: 373 22 294 079
Tel: 373 22 294 082
Fax: 373 22 293 596

Import/export control activity; establishment of legislative measures of control for manufacture or trade in illicit drugs.

Reunion — Réunion — Reunión

Articles 18, 16

Direction régionale des affaires sanitaires et sociales
Inspection des pharmacies
B.P. 50
97490 Sainte-Clotilde
Réunion
Tel: 262 939 414

Article 12

Mission nationale de Contrôle des Précurseurs
    Chimiques (MNCPC)
Direction Générale des Enterprises (DGE)
67 rue Barbès 94201 Ivry sur Seine Cedex
France
Tel: 33 1 7984 3169
Fax: 33 1 7984 3637
E-mail: mncpc@finances.gouv.fr

Romania — Roumanie — Rumania

Articles 18, 16

Ministry of Health
Cristian Popisteanu Street 1-3, District 1
010024 Bucharest
Romania
Tel: 40 21 307 25 47
Fax: 40 21 307 25 48
E-mail: andrei.bucsan@ms.ro

Articles 18, 16

Ministry of Internal Affairs
National Anti-Drug Agency
37 Unirii Boulevard, A4 ground floor, District 3
Bucharest
Romania
Tel: 40 21 323 30 30
Fax: 40 21 316 67 27
E-mail: monitorizare.oferta.droguri@ana.gov.ro

Responsible for statistical data related to drug supply reduction.

Articles 18, 16

Ministry of Internal Affairs
General Inspectorate of Romanian Police
General Directorate for the Countering Organized Crime
Anti-Drug Office
13-15 Stefan cel Mare Street, District 2
Bucharest
Romania
Tel: 40 21 208 25 25
Fax: 40 21 301 05 22
E-mail: antidrog@politiaromana.ro

Responsible for operational data related to drug trafficking.

Article 12

As regards legislation and coordination of administrative cooperation, please refer to entry of the European Union.

General Inspectorate of Romanian Police
General Directorate for the Countering Organized Crime
Anti-Drug Office
13-15 Stefan cel Mare Street
District 2
Bucharest
Romania
Tel: 40 21 310 0522
Fax: 40 21 310 0522
Fax: 40 21 311 05 28
E-mail: mihai.andrei@politiaromana.ro
E-mail: antidrog@politiaromana.ro

Responsible for control, investigations and stopping suspicious shipments.

Article 12

As regards legislation and coordination of administrative cooperation, please refer to entry of the European Union.

National Anti-Drug Agency
Ministry of Internal Affairs
37 Unirii Boulevard
A4, ground floor
3rd District
Bucharest
Romania
Tel: 40 21 314 76 77
Fax: 40 21 314 76 77
E-mail: rodica.mitoiu@ana.gov.ro
E-mail: precursori@ana.gov.ro

Responsible for monitoring the licit trade of precursors (administrative control of import and export of precursors; registration of companies dealing with precursors; issuance of import/export authorizations; entitled to give answers to inquiries on the legitimacy of Romanian operators; sends pre-export notifications to competent authorities of importing countries in order to verify the legitimacy of the transaction; receives and provides information on suspicious transactions and passes them to competent national authorities and to INCB.

Russian Federation — Fédération de Russie — Federación de Rusia

Articles 18, 16

Ministry of Industry and Trade
Kitaygorodsky Proezd 7
109074 Moscow
Russian Federation
Tel: 7 495 539 2166
Tel: 7 495 539 2187
Fax: 7 495 632 8783
E-mail: www.minpromtorg.gov.ru

Article 12

Ministry of Industry and Trade
Kitaygorodsky proezd 7
109074 Moscow
Russian Federation
Tel: 7 495 538 2187
Tel: 7 495 539 2166
Fax: 7 495 632 8783
Web: www.minpromtorg.gov.ru

Receiving pre-export notifications for Table I and Table II substances.

Russian Federation — Fédération de Russie — Federación de Rusia

(continued — suite — continuación)

Article 12

Ministry of Health and Social Development
Department of Pharmaceutical Development and
   Medical Equipment Markets
Rakhmanovsky per.3
127994 Moscow
Russian Federation
Tel: 7 495 606 1641
Fax: 7 495 606 1641

Receiving pre-export notifications for Table I substances.

Article 12(*)

Head, Department of International Cooperation
Federal Drug Control Service of the Russian Federation
12, Maroseika Street
101990 Moscow
Russian Federation
Tel: 7 495 625 3810
Tel: 7 495 621 6419
Fax: 7495 621 6419
Fax: 7 495 625 3774
E-mail: ums@gnk.gov.ru

Rwanda

Articles 18, 16

Pharmacy Task Force
Ministry of Health
P.O. Box 84
Kigali
Rwanda
Tel: 250 516 711
E-mail: Dirpharmacie@yahoo.fr

Article 12(*)

Directeur de la pharmacie
Ministère de la santé publique et des affaires sociales
B.P. 84
Kigali
Rwanda
Tel: 250 5 76556
Tel: 250 75968
Fax: 250 5 72904
Fax: 250 5 72902

Saint Helena — Sainte-Hélène — Santa Elena

Articles 18, 16

Senior Medical Officer, Clinical Director
Health and Social Services Directorate
Upper Jamestown
Saint Helena
STHL 1ZZ
South Atlantic Ocean
Tel: 290 22500

Article 12(*)

Chief Medical Officer, Public Health Directorate
Ministry of Public Health
General Hospital
Jamestown
Saint Helena
STHL 1ZZ
South Atlantic Ocean
Tel: 290 22500 ext 331
Fax: 290 22530
E-mail: smo@publichealth.gov.sh
E-mail: pharmacist@publichealth.gov.sh

Saint Kitts and Nevis — Saint-Kitts-et-Nevis — Saint Kitts y Nevis

Article 12(*)

Director of Health Services
Ministry of Health
Connell Street
P.O. Box 236
Basseterre
Saint Kitts and Nevis
Tel: 1 869 4652 5211 134
Tel: 1 869 4652 5211 085
Tel: 1 869 4652 5211 146
Fax: 1 869 4651 316
Fax: 1 869 466 8574

Article

Director of Health Services
Ministry of Health
Connell Street
P.O. Box 236
Basseterre
Saint Kitts and Nevis
Tel: 1 869 4652 5211 146
Tel: 1 869 4652 5211 085
Tel: 1 869 4652 5211 134
Fax: 1 869 4651 316
Fax: 1 869 4651 312

Saint Lucia — Sainte-Lucie — Santa Lucía

Article 12

Chief Medical Officer
Ministry of Health
Chaussee Road
Castries
Saint Lucia
Tel: 1 758 453 2668
Tel: 1 758 452 2589
Fax: 1 758 452 5655
Fax: 1 758 453 1080
E-mail: health@candw.lc

(Article not specified)

Chief Medical Officer
Ministry of Health
Chaussee Road
Castries
Saint Lucia
Tel: 1 758 453 2673
Fax: 1 758 453 1080
E-mail: health@candw.lc

Saint Pierre and Miquelon – Saint-Pierre-et-Miquelon – San Pedro y Miquelón

Articles 18, 16

Hospital of Saint Pierre and Miquelon
Pharmacy
Saint Pierre and Miquelon

Article 12

Mission nationale de Contrôle des Précurseurs
    Chimiques (MNCPC)
Direction Générale des Enterprises (DGE)
67 rue Barbès 94201 Ivry sur Seine Cedex
France
Tel: 33 1 7984 3169
Fax: 33 1 7984 3637
E-mail: mncpc@finances.gouv.fr

Saint Vincent and the Grenadines - Saint-Vincent-et-les-Grenadines - San Vicente y las Granadinas

Articles 18, 16

Ministry of Health and the Environment
Ministerial Building, 1st floor
Kingstown
Saint Vincent and the Grenadines
West Indies
Tel: 1 784 457 1612
Fax: 1 784 457 2684
E-mail: mohesvg@vinciusurf.com

Article 12(*)

Permanent Secretary
Ministry of Health and the Environment
Ministerial Building
Kingstown
Saint Vincent and the Grenadines
Tel: 1 784 456 1111 ext. 511/512
Fax: 1 784 457 2684
E-mail: mohesvg@vincysurf.com

Samoa

Article 12

Director of Pharmaceutical Services
Department of Health
Private Bag Motootua
Apia
Samoa
Tel: 685 21212
Fax: 685 22905
Fax: 685 24610

(Article not specified)

Director-General of Health
Health Department
P.O. Box 192
Apia
Samoa
Tel: 685 21212
Fax: 685 24610

San Marino — Saint-Marin — San Marino

Articles 18, 16

Secrétariat d'État aux affaires étrangères
Contrada Omerelli
Saint-Marin
Tel: 378 885 795
Fax: 378 992 018

Sao Tome and Principe — Sao Tomé-et-Principe — Santo Tomé y Príncipe

Articles 18, 16

Ministère de la santé
B.P. 23
Sao Tomé
Sao Tomé-et-Principe
Tel: 239 12 21359

Article 12(*)

Directeur, Direction de la pharmacie
Ministère de la santé
B.P. 23
Sao Tomé
Sao Tomé-et-Principe
Tel: 239 12 22290

Saudi Arabia — Arabie saoudite — Arabia Saudita

Articles 18, 16

Saudi Food and Drug Authority
Narcotic Drug Department
Al-Nafl District
P.O. Box 6288
Riyadh 13312
Kingdom of Saudi Arabia
Tel: 966 11 203 8222 ext. 5712
Fax: 966 11 205 7630
E-mail: narcotic.drug@sfda.gov.sa

Article 12

Director
General Directorate of Narcotics Control
Ministry of Interior
P.O. Box 2538
Riyadh 11461
Saudi Arabia
Tel: 966 11 462 9393
Fax: 966 11 461 4231
E-mail: Gdnc-ksa@gdnc.gov.sa

Law enforcement.

Article 12

Saudi Food and Drug Authority
Saudi Food and Drug Authority
SFDA-3292
North Highway AlNafa
Riyadh 13312-6288
Kingdom of Saudi Arabia
Tel: 966 1 1 203 8222 EXT. 5712
Fax: 966 11 205 7630
E-mail: narcotic.drug@sfda.gov.sa

Issues import/export authorizations.

Senegal — Sénégal

Articles 18, 16

Direction de la pharmacie et des laboratoires
Ministère de la santé publique
153 Rue Mousse Diop
B.P. 6150
Dakar
Sénégal
Tel: 221 822 4470
Fax: 221 821 0910
E-mail: ctdieye@yahoo.fr

Article 12

Directeur de la Police judiciaire
Service des statistiques et des informations (DPS)
DGSN/MINT
Dakar
Sénégal
Tel: 221 9224

Article 12

Directeur du Bureau de contrôle et de visas
153, rue Mousse Diop
Dakar
Sénégal
Tel: 221 338 2244 70
Fax: 221 338 2109 10
E-mail: ctdieye@yahoo.fr

Serbia — Serbie

Articles 18, 16

Ministry of Health
Sector for Medicines and Medical Devices
Department for Narcoitic Drugs and Precursors (Narcotic
   Drug Services)
Nemanjina 22-26
11000 Belgrade
Serbia
Tel: 381 11 260 7941
Fax: 381 11 260 7941
E-mail: d.kosic@zdravlje.sr.gov.rs

Article 12

Head, Narcotic Drugs Service
Ministry of Health
1, Omladinskih Brigada Street
11070 Belgrade
Serbia
Tel: 381 11 311 2381
Fax: d.kosic@zdravlje.sr.gov.rs
Fax: 381 11 260 7941
Fax: 381 11 311 7550
E-mail: dusan.ilic@zdravlje.gov.rs

Article 12

Head, National Central Bureau of INTERPOL
Ministry of Interior
Terazije 41
11000 Belgrade
Serbia
Tel: 381 11 334 5254
Fax: 381 11 334 6822
Fax: 381 11 334 6142
E-mail: office@interpolbelgrade.gov.rs

Investigation and law enforcement.

Seychelles

Articles 18, 16

Public Health Commissioner
Public Health Department
Ministry of Health
Seychelles Hospital
P.O. Box 52, Mont Fleuri
Mahé
Seychelles
Tel: 248 4 388 000
Fax: 248 4 225 131
E-mail: jgedeon@health.gov.sc

Article 12(*)

Principal Secretary
Ministry of Health
P.O. Box 52, Victoria Hospital
Mahé
Seychelles
Tel: 248 388 000
Fax: 248 224 792
E-mail: bvalentin@health.gov.sc

Sierra Leone

Articles 18, 16

Pharmacy Board of Sierra Leone
C/O Pharmacy Board of Sierra Leone
Central Medical Stores, New England
Freetown, Sierra Leone
West Africa
Tel: 232 76 834 895
E-mail: manndulai@yahoo.co.uk
E-mail: pharmbdsl@hotmail.com

Article 12(*)

Chairman, Pharmacy Board
64, Siaka Stevens Street, P.M.B. 322
Freetown
Sierra Leone
Tel: 232 222 8497
Tel: 232 229 346
Fax: 232 224 526

Issues import authorizations for ephedrine.

Singapore — Singapour — Singapur

Articles 18, 16

Health Sciences Authority
150 Cantonment Road
Cantonment Centre
Blk A, #01-02
Singapore 089762
Singapore
Tel: 65 6866 3522
Fax: 65 6478 9068
E-mail: HSA_certification@hsa.gov.sg

Article 12

Director, Central Narcotics Bureau
Ministry of Home Affairs
393 New Bridge Road
Singapore 088763
Singapore
Tel: 65 6325 1184
Fax: 65 6227 3979
E-mail: CNB_Chemical_Enquiry@cnb.gov.sg

Coordinating body for implementation of article 12 of the 1988 Convention; issues import and export authorizations for substances in Table I and Table II; investigation and law enforcement.

Sint Maarten — Saint-Martin (partie néerlandaise) — San Martín

Articles 18, 16

Inspector-General of Public Health
Inspectorate of Public Health
APNA-Plaza
Building E (3rd floor)
Schouwburgweg 24-26
P.O. Box 3824
Curaçao
Tel: 599 9 466 9366
Fax: 599 9 466 9367
E-mail: peter.fontilus@gov.an

On 10 October 2010, the Netherlands Antilles officially ceased to exist. Curaçao and Sint Maarten have become two new constituent entities.

Sint Maarten — Saint-Martin (partie néerlandaise) — San Martín
(continued — suite — continuación)

Article 12

Acting Inspector of Pharmaceutical Affairs
Inspectorate of Pharmaceutical Affairs
Inspectorate of Health, Environment and Nature
P.O. Box 3824
Curaçao
Tel: 599 9 466 9366
Fax: 599 9 466 9367
E-mail: cleopatra.hazel@curacao-gov.an

On 10 October 2010, the Netherlands Antilles officially ceased to exist. Curaçao and Sint Maarten have become two new constituent entities.

Slovakia — Slovaquie — Eslovaquia

Articles 18, 16

Ministry of Health
Department of Pharmacy
Limbová 2
837 52 Bratislava
Slovakia
Tel: 421 2 5937 3553
Tel: 421 2 5937 3230
Fax: 421 2 5477 6048
E-mail: martina.hromadkova@health.gov.sk
E-mail: jozef.slany@health.gov.sk

Article 12

As regards legislation and coordination of administrative cooperation, please refer to entry of the European Union.

Director General
Section of Pharmacy and Medicines Policy
Ministry of Health
Limbová 2
837 52 Bratislava
Slovakia
Tel: 421 2 5937 3364
Tel: 421 2 5937 3111 (Switchboard)
Fax: 421 2 5477 7983
Fax: 421 2 5477 6048
E-mail: Adam.Hloska@health.gov.sk

Article 12

As regards legislation and coordination of administrative cooperation, please refer to entry of the European Union.

Director, Department of Trade Measures
Ministry of Economy
Mierová 19
827 15 Bratislava
Slovakia
Tel: 421 2 4854 2175
Fax: 421 2 4342 3915
E-mail: Silvia.Horvathova@economy.gov.sk
E-mail: shorvathova@mhsr.sk

Regulatory responsibilities for the implementation of article 12 of 1988 Convention. Receives pre-export notifications for all Table I substances, anthranilic acid, phenylacetic acid and piperidine.

Article 12

As regards legislation and coordination of administrative cooperation, please refer to entry of the European Union.

Ministry of Interior of the Slovak Republic
Police Force Headquarters
National Criminal Agency
National Drug Enforcement Unit
Pribinova 2
812 72 Bratislava
Slovakia
Tel: 421 9610 54501
Fax: 421 9610 59001
E-mail: precursors@minv.sk
E-mail: npdj@minv.sk

Law enforcement.

Slovenia — Slovénie — Eslovenia

Articles 18, 16

Agency for Medical Products and Medical Devices
Ptujska 21
1000 Ljubljana
Slovenia
Tel: 386 8 2000 500
Fax: 386 8 2000 510
E-mail: info@jazmp.si

Article 12

As regards legislation and coordination of administrative cooperation, please refer to entry of the European Union.

National Chemicals Bureau
Ministry of Health
Ajdovšcina 4
1000 Ljubljana
Slovenia
Tel: 386 1 478 6051
Fax: 386 1 478 6266
E-mail: gp-ursk.mz@gov.si

Surveillance of traffic of narcotic drugs, psychotropic substances and precursors. Legislation, licensing, import/export authorization.

Article 12

Ministry of the Interior
Stefanova 2
61001 Ljubljana
Slovenia
Tel: 386 1 132 5125
Tel: 386 1 125 1400
Fax: 386 1 251 7516

Control and investigation.

Solomon Islands — Îles Salomon — Islas Salomón

Articles 18, 16

Permanent Secretary
Ministry of Health and Medical Services
Honiara
Solomon Islands

Article 12

Director of National Pharmacy Services, (Government Pharmacist)
Regulatory Affairs Unit
National Pharmacy Services Division
P.O. Box 349
Honiara
Solomon Islands
Tel: 677 30890
Fax: 677 30891
E-mail: govpharmacy@solomon.com.sb

Somalia — Somalie

(Article not specified)

Pharmaceutical Department
Ministry of Health
P.O. Box 1750
Mogadiscio
Somalia

South Africa — Afrique du Sud— Sudáfrica

Articles 18, 16

The Registrar of Medicines
Department of Health
Private Bag X828
Pretoria 0001
South Africa
Tel: 27 12 312 0286
Tel: 27 12 312 0000
Fax: 27 12 326 4382

Article 12

The Commander, South African Police Service
Chemical Monitoring Programme
Private Bag X302
Pretoria 0001
South Africa
Tel: 27 12 393 1942
Tel: 27 12 393 2240
Fax: 27 12 393 1948
Fax: 27 12 393 1953
E-mail: clarkeav@saps.org.za

Law enforcement.

Spain — Espagne — España

Articles 18, 16

Área de Estupefacientes y Psicotrópos
Subdirección General de Inspección y Control de
   Medicamentos
Agencia Española de Medicamentos y Productos
   Sanitarios
C/Campezo No. 1
Edificio 8
28022 Madrid
España
Tel: 34 91 822 5224
Tel: 34 91 822 5237
Fax: 34 91 822 5243
E-mail: sgicm@aemps.es

Spain — Espagne — España
(continued — suite — continuación)

Article 12

As regards legislation and coordination of administrative cooperation, please refer to entry of the European Union.

Brigada Central de Estupefacientes, Dirección General
  de la Policía
Sección de Precursores y Sinéticos
Ministerio del Interior
C/Julián González Segador s/n
Madrid 28043
España
Tel: 34 91 582 2554
Tel: 34 91 582 2546
Fax: 34 91 300 3903
E-mail: jgc.uce@policia.es

Investigation of offences.

Article 12

As regards legislation and coordination of administrative cooperation, please refer to entry of the European Union.

Agencia   Estatal   de   Administración   Tributaria
Departamento de Aduanas e II.EE Impuestos Especiales
Dirección Adjunta de Vigilancia Aduanera
Unidad de Precursores
Avda. Del Llano Castellano, 17
28071 Madrid
España
Tel: 34 91 728 9914
Tel: 34 91 728 9507
Fax: 34 91 358 3417
E-mail: Precursores.adu@correo.aeat.es

Licensing, registration and import/export authorizations; control and investigation.

Article 12

As regards legislation and coordination of administrative cooperation, please refer to entry of the European Union.

Centro de Inteligencia Contra el Terrorismo y el Crimen
  Organizado (CITCO)
Ministerio del Interior
Área de Precursores
Secretaria de Estado de Seguridad
Calle Josefa Valcárcel, 28-5a planta
28071 Madrid
España
Tel: 34 91 537 2766
Fax: 34 91 537 2722
E-mail: precursores@interior.es

Coordination, license, registration and monitoring of EU internal trade.

Article 12

As regards legislation and coordination of administrative cooperation, please refer to entry of the European Union.

Dirección General de la Guardia Civil
Jefatura de Policía Judicial
Unidad Técnica de Policía Judicial
Grupo de Drogas, Precursores y Consumo
C/Principe de Vergara, 246
28016 Madrid
Spain
Tel: 34 91 514 6122
Fax: 34 91 514 6284
E-mail: 34 91 514 6265
E-mail: utpj-reg@guardiacivil.es

Sri Lanka

Article 18

Medical Supplies Division
357, Deans Road
Colombo 10
Sri Lanka
Tel: 94 1 694 111
Fax: 94 1 697 096

Article 16

Cosmetics Drugs and Devices Authority
Ministry of Health
120, Norris Canal Road
Colombo 10
Sri Lanka
Tel: 94 1 695 173
Fax: 94 1 689 704

Article 12

Chairperson
Precursor Control Authority
Affiliated to the National Dangerous Drugs Control Board
Ministry of Defence
383 Kotte Road, Rajagiriya
Sri Lanka
Tel: 94 11 286 8794-6
Fax: 94 11 286 9805
Fax: 94 11 286 8792
Fax: 94 11 286 8791
E-mail: pca@nddcb.gov.lk
E-mail: mail@nddcb.gov.lk

Issue of import certificates for ephedrine preparations. Issue of licenses for manufacture of ephedrine preparations.

Sudan — Soudan — Sudán

Articles 18, 16

National Medicine and Poisons Board
Khartoum
Sudan
Tel: 249 155 883 318
Tel: 249 155 880 271
Fax: 249 183 522 263
E-mail: info@nmpb.gov.sd
E-mail: nmpb.nar@hotmail.com

Article 12

Secretary General
National Medicines and Poisons Board
Secretariat General
Khartoum 60 street
Sudan
Tel: 249 155 880270
Tel: 249 9122 10674
E-mail: nmpb.100@gmail.com
E-mail: info@nmpb.gov.sd

Issue import/export certificates under the international drug control.

Suriname

Articles 18, 16

Director of Health
Gravenstraat 64
Paramaribo
Suriname
Tel: 597 477 601
Fax: 597 473 923

Article 12

Head, Judicial Department
Police Force of Suriname
Detective Department
Havenlaan
Nieuwe Haven
Paramaribo
Suriname
Tel: 597 0366 110 (Home)
Tel: 597 473 101 (Office)
Tel: 597 403 608 (Office)
Fax: 597 402 535

Receives and replies to queries on legitimacy of transactions involving chemicals.

Article 12

National Anti-Drugs Council
Gravenstraat 64
Paramaribo
Suriname
Tel: 597 472 923
Fax: 597 477 109
E-mail: narsur@sr.net

Overall coordination.

Article 12

Head, Division of Import/Export and Foreign Currency Control
Detective Department
Ministry of Trade and Industry
Havenlaan
Nieuwe Haven
Paramaribo
Suriname
Tel: 597 403 440
Tel: 597 402 889
Fax: 597 402 602

Issuing or refusing import/export licenses for chemicals mentioned on the negative list.

Article 12(*)

Director of Health
Ministry of Health
Gravenstraat 64
Paramaribo
Suriname
Tel: 597 477 601
Fax: 597 473 923

Control of import and export of chemicals.

Swaziland — Swazilandia

Articles 18, 16

Health Specialist
Ministry of Health
P.O. Box 5
Mbabane
Swaziland
Tel: 268 7606 2705
Tel: 268 2404 5554
Fax: 268 2404 7420
E-mail: magagulasam@gov.sz

Article 12

Director of Health Services
Ministry of Health
P.O. Box 5
Mbabane
Swaziland
Tel: 268 404 4345
Tel: 268 404 4090
Tel: 268 404 5514
Tel: 268 404 5991
Tel: 268 404 2431
Tel: 268 604 0041 (mobile)
Tel: 268 404 4016
Fax: 268 404 2092

Issuing import/export authorizations.

Sweden — Suède — Suecia

Articles 18, 16

Medical Products Agency
P.O. Box 26
75103 Uppsala
Sweden
Tel: 46 18 174 600
Fax: 46 18 548 566
E-mail: registrator@mpa.se

Article 12

As regards legislation and coordination of administrative cooperation, please refer to entry of the European Union.

Medical Products Agency
Dag Hammarskjölds väg 42
P.O. Box 26
S-75103 Uppsala
Sweden
Tel: 46 18 174 600
Fax: 46 18 548 566
E-mail: registrator@mpa.se

General functions: Coordination, control licit trade. Specific functions: Issues licenses/and export authorizations. Registers operators. Supervises the legal handling of precursors. Collects data on licit trade. Replies to inquiries.

Article 12

As regards legislation and coordination of administrative cooperation, please refer to entry of the European Union.

Swedish Customs
Head Office
P.O. Box 12854
S-112 98 Stockholm
Sweden
Tel: 46 8 4050570 (24 hours)
Fax: 46 8 6540611
E-mail: ncp@customs.se

General functions: Import and export control. Investigation of contravention of customs law/law enforcement. Specific functions: Investigation of suspicious orders, controlled deliveries.

Switzerland — Suisse — Suiza

Articles 18, 16, 12

Swissmedic
Swiss Agency for Therapeutic Products
Narcotics Division
Hallerstrasse 7
3000 Bern 9
Switzerland
Tel: 41 31 322 04 89
Tel: 41 31 324 91 87
E-mail: monika.joos@swissmedic.ch
E-mail: narcotics@swissmedic.ch

CNA for article 12, 1988 Convention: Registration, import/export licences, etc.

Article 12

Office fédéral de la Police
Nussbaumstrasse 29
3003 Berne
Suisse
Tel: 41 31 322 44 51
Tel: 41 31 322 44 50
Fax: 41 31 312 31 80
Fax: 41 31 322 53 04

Point central de contact. Renforcement de la loi, trafic illicite.

Syrian Arab Republic — République arabe syrienne — República Árabe Siria

Articles 18, 16

Ministry of Health, Pharmaceutical Affairs Directorate
Drugs Section
Ministry of Health
Meissat Compound
Damascus
Syrian Arab Republic
Tel: 963 1274 0650
Fax: 963 1275 6763
E-mail: dpa.dru@moh.gov.sy

Article 12

Director
Directorate of Pharmaceutical Affairs
Ministry of Health
Al-Nejmah Square
Damascus
Syrian Arab Republic
Tel: 963 11 275 8114
Fax: 963 11 333 0542
Fax: 963 11 275 6763
E-mail: dpa.dir@moh.gov.sy

Tajikistan – Tadjikistan – Tayikistán

Articles 18, 16

Head
Unit of Specially Controlled Substances
Ministry of Health
Ul. Navoi 5/5
Dushanbe
Tajikistan
Tel: 992 372 222 5237
Tel: 992 372 221 3064
Fax: 992 372 227 6569

Article 12

Director, Drug Control Agency under the President of the
   Republic of Tajikistan
UL.N. Karabaeva, 52
734000 Dushanbe
Tajikistan
Tel: 992 372 233 8475
Tel: 992 372 234 8129
Fax: 992 372 234 8129
E-mail: kzon@akn.tj
E-mail: dca@tojikiston.com

Licenses import, export, manufacture, sale and trade in
precursors.

Article 12(*)

National Scientific Centre for Expertise
Techron Street 12
734025 Dushanbe
Tajikistan
Tel: 992 372 217 750

Thailand — Thaïlande — Tailandia

Articles 18, 16

Food and Drug Administration
Ministry of Public Health
Tiwanon Road
Nonthaburi 11000
Thailand
Tel: 66 2 590 7332
Tel: 66 2 590 7346
Fax: 66 2 590 7345
Fax: 66 2 591 8471
E-mail: narcotic@fda.moph.go.th

Article 12

The Secretary-General, Office of the Narcotics Control
   Board
Office of the Prime Minister
Din Daeng Road
Phyathal
Bangkok 10400
Thailand
Tel: 66 2 245 9073
Tel: 66 2 245 9072
Tel: 66 2 245 9071
Fax: 66 2 640 9900
Fax: 66 2 245 9354
E-mail: Soponh@Mozart.Inet.Co.Th

Article 12

Suppression of illicit traffic
The Secretary-General, Food and Drug Administration
Ministry of Public Health
Tiwanon Road
Nonthaburi 11000
Thailand
Tel: 66 2 590 7332
Tel: 66 2 590 7341
Fax: 66 2 590 7345
Fax: 66 2 591 8471
Fax: 66 2 591 8636
E-mail: narcotic@fda.moph.go.th

Import/export authorizations for: ephedrine, ergotamine,
ergometrine, pseudoephedrine and acetic anhydride.

Article 12

Narcotics Suppression Bureau
Police Department
Rama I Road
Pathumwan District
Bangkok 10330
Thailand
Tel: 66 2 251 7966
Fax: 66 2 251 2726

Suppression of illicit traffic.

Article 12

Customs Department
Sunthornkosa Road
Klong Toey
Bangkok 10110
Thailand
Tel: 66 2 494 021
Fax: 66 2 494 043

Article 12

Controls imports and exports of chemicals
Director-General, Department of Industrial Works
Ministry of Industry
7516 Rama VI Road
Bangkok 10400
Thailand
Tel: 66 2 202 4005
Tel: 66 2 202 4012-4
Fax: 66 2 202 4015

Issues import/export licenses for acetone, methyl ethyl
ketone (MEK), toluene, sulphuric acid, hydrochloric acid.

Thailand — Thaïlande — Tailandia
(continued — suite — continuación)

Article 12

Director-General, Department of Internal Trade
Ministry of Commerce
Maharat Road
Bangkok 10200
Thailand
Tel: 66 2 219 891
Fax: 66 2 219 891

Controls the transfer of ether and chloroform.

The former Yugoslav Republic of Macedonia —
L'Ex-République yougoslave de Macédonie —
La ex República Yugoslava de Macedonia

Articles 18, 16

Sector for Controlled Substances, Bureau for Medicines
Ministry of Health
Ul. Vodnjanska bb
1000 Skopje
The form. Yug. Rep. of Macedonia
Tel: 389 2 3112 500 ext. 127
Fax: 389 2 3298 435
E-mail: tanja.petrusevska@gmail.com

Article 12(*)

President, Narcotic Drugs and Psychotropic Substances
  Commission
Ministry of Health
Vodnjanska b.b.
91 000 Skopje
The form. Yug. Rep. of Macedonia
Tel: 389 2 3113 429
Fax: 389 2 3113 014

Timor-Leste

Article 12

Minister for Foreign Affairs and Cooperation, Ministry of
Foreign Affairs, Palacio do Governo, Dili, Timor-Leste
through/copy: Permanent Mission of Timor-Leste to the
United
Nations (New York)
866 Second Avenue, 9th Floor
New York, N.Y. 10017
U.S.A.
Tel: 1 212 759 3675
Fax: 1 212 759 4196
E-mail: Timor-Leste@un.int

Togo

Articles 18, 16

Direction des pharmacies, laboratoires et équipements
  techniques (DPLET)
Ministère de la santé
B.P. 386
Lomé
Togo
Tel: 228 920 62 21
Tel: 228 221 38 01
E-mail: dpmtogo@yahoo.fr
E-mail: bnyansa@yahoo.fr

Article 12

Directeur des pharmacies, Laboratoires et équipements
  techniques
Direction générale de la santé publique
B.P. 336
Lomé
Togo
Tel: 228 222 07 99
Tel: 228 221 38 01
Tel: 228 222 20 73
Fax: 228 221 38 01
Fax: 228 222 20 73

Tonga

Articles 18, 16

The Prime Minister
P.O. Box 62
Nuku'Alofa
Tonga
Tel: 676 24644
Fax: 676 23888

Article 12

Minister for Police
Office of the Minister of Police, Prisons
  and Fire Services
P.O. Box 8
Nuku'Alofa
Tonga
Tel: 676 24815
Fax: 676 28122
E-mail: sttuutafaiva@gmail.com

Article 12

Commander of Police
P.O. Box 8
Nuku'Alofa
Tonga
Tel: 676 23233
Fax: 676 23226

Article 12

Officer-in-charge, Criminal Investigation Department
P.O. Box 8
Nuku'Alofa
Tonga
Tel: 676 23233
Fax: 676 23226

Trinidad and Tobago — Trinité-et-Tobago —Trinidad y Tobago

Articles 18, 16

Chief Medical Officer
63, Park Street
Port of Spain
Trinidad and Tobago
Tel: 1 868 627 0010/14 ext. 1617
Tel: 1 868 627 0010/14 ext. 1616
Fax: 1 868 623 3755
E-mail: cmo@health.gov.tt

Article 12

Chief Medical Officer
Ministry of Health
63, Park Street
Port of Spain
Trinidad and Tobago
Tel: 1 868 627 0010/14 ext.1616
Fax: 1 868 623 3755
E-mail: colin.furlonge@health.gov.tt

Tunisia —Tunisie — Túnez

Articles 18, 16

Direction de la pharmacie et du médicament
Ministère de la santé
31, rue Khartoum
Tunis 1035
Tunisie
Tel: 216 71 795 250
Tel: 216 71 796 824
Fax: 216 71 797 816
Fax: 216 71 795 250

Article 12(*)

Le Directeur général, Direction de la pharmacie et du
  médicament
Ministère de la santé
31, rue Khartoum
Tunis 1035
Tunisie
Tel: 216 71 796 824
Tel: 216 71 795 250
Fax: 216 71 797 816

Turkey — Turquie — Turquía

Articles 18, 16

Ministry of Health Turkish Medicines and Medical
  Devices Agency
Sö ütözü Mahallesi. 2176 Sokak No.5
06520 Çankaya
ANKARA
Tel: 90 312 218 3316
Fax: 90 312 218 3290
E-mail: demet.aydink@titck.gov.tr

Article 12

Director
Risk Management Department
Turkish Medicines and Medical Devices Agency
Ministry of Health
Sögütözü Mahallesi 2176
Sokak No.5
Çankaya/Ankara
Turkey
Tel: 90 312 218 3316
Fax: 90 312 218 3290
E-mail: demet.aydink@titck.gov.tr

Registration, import/export licenses, receipt of pre-export notifications. Responsible for all stages of legal trade of all the substances listed in the schedules to the 1961,1971 and 1988 Convention as well as their preparations

Turkmenistan — Turkménistan — Turkmenistán

Articles 18, 16, 12

State Service of Turkmenistan for the Protection of Public
  Health
Ul. 2023, dom 9
Ashgabat, 744000
Turkmenistan
Tel: 9931 2931 083
Fax: 9931 2931 152
E-mail: sstpshs@online.tm

Issuing permits for import and export to/from Turkmenistan of narcotics drugs, psychotropic substances and precursors.

Article 12(*)

The Minister of Health
Ministry of Health and Medical Industries
96, Mahtumkuli Prospect
Ashkhabad 744006
Turkmenistan
Tel: 993 1 235 5834
Tel: 993 1 235 1063
Fax: 993 1 235 5032

Turks and Caicos Islands — Îles Turques et Caïques — Islas Turcas y Caicos

Articles 18, 16

Chief Medical Officer
Grand Turk Hospital
Grand Turk
Turks and Caicos Islands
Tel: 1 809 2586
Tel: 1 809 2040

Tuvalu

Articles 18, 16

Senior Medical Officer
Princess Margaret Hospital
Funafuti
Tuvalu
Tel: 751 688 751

Article 12(*)

The Director of Health
Ministry of Health and Human Resources Development
P.O. Box 36
Funafuti
Tuvalu

Uganda — Ouganda

Articles 18, 16

National Drug Authority
Plot 46-48, Lumumba Avenue
P.O. Box 23096
Kampala
Uganda
Tel: 256 41 255 665
Fax: 256 41 255 758
E-mail: ndaug@nda.or.ug

Article 12

Executive Director, National Drug Authority
Secretariat Office
Plot 46-48 Lumumba Avenue
P.O. Box 23096
Kampala
Uganda
Tel: 256 41 434 7392
Tel: 256 41 425 5665
Tel: 256 41 434 7391
Fax: 256 41 425 5758
E-mail: ndaug@nda.or.ug

Licensing, issuing import and export authorizations.

Ukraine — Ucrania

Articles 18, 16

State Service on Drugs Control
Prospect Chervonozoryanyi 51
03680 Kiev
Ukraine
Tel: 380 44 275 6814
Fax: 380 44 275 4287
E-mail: info@narko.gov.ua
Web: www.narko.gov.ua

Article 12

Head
State Service on Drugs Control
Prospect Chervonozorryanyi 51
03680 Kiev
Ukraine
Tel: 380 44 275 6814
Fax: 380 44 275 4287
E-mail: info@narko.gov.ua
Web: www.narko.gov.ua

United Arab Emirates — Emirats arabes unis — Emiratos Árabes Unidos

Articles 18, 16

Registration and Drug Control Department
Ministry of Health
Sheikh Hamdan Street
Al Otaiba Tower
P.O. Box 848
Abu Dhabi
United Arab Emirates
Tel: 971 2 611 7389
Tel: 971 2 611 7421
Fax: 971 2 631 3742
E-mail: albraiki2@yahoo.com

Article 12

Federal Director, Drug Control Department
Ministry of Health
P.O. Box 848
Abu Dhabi
United Arab Emirates
Tel: 971 2 621 1357
Tel: 971 2 633 0000
Fax: 971 2 631 3742

Article 12

Director-General, Dubai Ports Customs
P.O. Box 63
Dubai
United Arab Emirates
Tel: 971 4 345 9575
Fax: 971 4 345 2002
Fax: 971 4 345 0934

Article 12

Federal General Department of Anti-Narcotics
Precursors & Chemicals Control Section
Ministry of Interior
Airport Road, Zayed Sport City
P.O. Box 398
Abu Dhabi
United Arab Emirates
Tel: 971 2 402 3163
Fax: 971 2 441 4633
Fax: 971 2 441 4688
E-mail: Dea_khalid@moi.gov.ae

Law enfoncement.

United Kingdom of Great Britain and Northern Ireland — Royaume-Uni (de Grande-Bretagne et d'Irlande du Nord) — Reino Unido (de Gran Bretaña e Irlanda del Norte)

Articles 18, 16

Home Office
Drug Licensing and Compliance Unit
2 Marsham Street
London SW1P 4DF
United Kingdom
Tel: 44 20 7035 6330
E-mail: Adam.Spriggs@homeoffice.gsi.gov.uk
E-mail: DLCUCommsOfficer@homeoffice.gsi.gov.uk
E-mail: Sarah.Muir@homeoffice.gsi.gov.uk
E-mail: Angharad.Thomas@homeoffice.gsi.gov.uk

Article 12

Head of Division
Drug Licensing and Compliance Unit
Drugs and Alcohol Unit
Home Office
4th Floor, Fry Building
2 Marsham Street, London SW1P 4DF
United Kingdom
Tel: 44 207 035 0771
Tel: 44 207 035 6330
Fax: 44 20 7035 6161
E-mail: Angharad.Steff@homeoffice.gsi.gov.uk
E-mail: licensingenquiry.aadu@homeoffice.gsi.gov.uk
E-mail: Christopher.Packham4@homeoffice.gsi.gov.uk
E-mail: Sarah.Muir@homeoffice.gsi.gov.uk
E-mail: Jill.Frankham@homeoffice.gsi.gov.uk
Web: www.drugs.homeoffice.gov.uk

Legislation and issuance of licenses.

Article 12

As regards legislation and coordination of administrative cooperation, please refer to entry of the European Union.

National Crime Agency
P.O. Box 8000
London SE11 5EN
United Kingdom
Tel: 44 370 496 7622

Law enforcement and seizures.

United Republic of Tanzania — République-Unie de Tanzanie — República Unida de Tanzanía

Articles 18, 16

Tanzania Food and Drugs Authority (TFDA)
P.O. Box 77150
Dar-es-Salaam
United Republic of Tanzania
Tel: 255 22 2450 512
Fax: 255 22 2452 108
E-mail: info@tfda.or.tz

Article 12(*)

Tanzania Food and Drugs Authority (TFDA)
Ministry of Health
P.O. Box 77150
Epi-Mabibo
Dar Es Salaam
United Republic of Tanzania
Tel: 255 22 2450 512
Tel: 255 22 2450 751
Fax: 255 22 2450 793
E-mail: hiiti.sillo@tfda.or.tz
E-mail: tfda@twiga.com

United States of America — Etats-Unis d'Amérique — Estados Unidos de América

Articles 18, 16

Deputy Assistant Administrator, Office of Diversion
  Control
Drug Enforcement Administration
8701 Morrissette Drive
Springfield, VA 22152-1080
United States of America
Tel: 1 202 307 7165

United States of America — Etats-Unis d'Amérique — Estados Unidos de América

(continued — suite — continuación)

Article 12

Deputy Assistant Administrator, Office of Diversion
  Control
Drug Enforcement Administration
8701 Morrissette Drive
Springfield, VA 22152-1080
United States of America
Tel: 1 202 307 7165

Receives pre-export notifications.

United States Virgin Islands — Îles Vierges américaines — Islas Vírgenes de los E.E.U.U.

See information immediately under United States of
America, Articles 18, 16

Uruguay

Articles 18, 16

División Sustancias Controladas
Dirección General de la Salud
Ministerio de Salud Pública
Convención 1366 Piso 2, Galería Caubarrere
Montevideo
Uruguay
Tel: 598 2 150 2334
Tel: 598 2 150 2332
Tel: 598 2 150 2205
Fax: 598 2 402 8032 106
E-mail: apla@msp.gub.uy

Article 12

Jefe, División Sustancias Controladas
Dirección General de la Salud
Ministerio de Salud Pública
Convención 1366 Piso 2, Galería Caubarrere
Montevideo
Uruguay
Tel: 598 2150 2332
Tel: 598 2150 2205
Tel: 598 2150 2334
Fax: 598 2402 8032 106
E-mail: apla@msp.gub.uy

Issues import certificate for ephedrine, ergotamine,
norephedrine and pseudoephedrine.

Article 12

Presidencia de la República
Prosecretaría de la Presidencia
Junta Nacional de Drogas
Edificio Torre Ejecutiva
Plaza Independencia 710, Piso 11
Montevideo
Uruguay
Tel: 598 2150 3908
Fax: 598 2917 1130
E-mail: prosecretaria@presidencia.gub.uy

Uzbekistan — Ouzbékistan — Uzbekistán

Articles 18, 16

Drug Control Committee
Central Directorate for Quality Control of Medicines and
  Medical Equipment
Ministry of Health
Proezd K. Umarova 16
ul. Ozod, Almar district
100002 Tashkent
Uzbekistan
Tel: 998 71 242 8459
Fax: 998 71 242 8459
E-mail: uzkomitet@rambler.ru

Article 12(*)

Head, Department of Drug and Medical Equipment,
  Quality Control, Licit Drugs Control Committee
Ministry of Public Health
16 K. Umarov Passage
Ozod Str., Almazar district
100002 Tashkent
Uzbekistan
Tel: 998 71 2 242 8459
Tel: 998 71 2 242 4893
Fax: 998 71 2 242 8459
E-mail: munira.shokhobova@minzdrav.uz
E-mail: uzkomitet@rambler.ru

Issuance of licenses, permits to import and export
substances included in Tables I and/or II

Article 12(*)

National Informational and Analytical Studies, Centre for
  Drug Control
Cabinet of Ministers
pl. Mustakillik 5
700000 Tashkent
Uzbekistan
Tel: 998 71 139 1063
Fax: 998 71 139 1063

Vanuatu

Article 12(*)

Principal Pharmacist
Department of Health
PMB 101
Port-Vila
Vanuatu
Tel: 678 24417
Fax: 678 24420

Venezuela (Bolivarian Republic of) – Venezuela (République bolivarienne du) – Venezuela (República Bolivariana de)

Articles 18, 16

Servicio Autónomo de Contraloría Sanitaria, Ministerio del Poder Popular para la Salud
Edificio Sur
Centro Simón Bolivar, Piso 3
Oficina 335, El Silencio
Caracas 1010
Venezuela (República Bolivariana de)
Tel: 58 212 408 0518
Fax: 58 212 408 0505

Article 12

Jefe, Departamento de Sustancias Psicotrópicas y Estupefacientes
Ministerio de Salud y Desarrollo Social (MSDS)
Edif. Sur, Centro Simón Bolívar, Piso 3, Ofic. 325
Caracas 1010
Venezuela (República Bolivariana de)
Tel: 58 212 481 5740
Tel: 58 212 481 9603
Tel: 58 212 482 3926
Fax: 58 212 975 4106
Fax: 58 212 482 2393

Control of Table I substances. Receives pre-export notifications for Table I substances.

Article 12

Jefe, Departamento de Competitividad
Ministerio de Industria y Comercio
Caracas
Venezuela (República Bolivariana de)
Tel: 58 212 761 7294
Fax: 58 212 762 9303
Fax: 58 212 762 9864

Control of Table II substances.

Article 12

Oficina Nacional Antidrogas
Edificio ONA, Av. Venezuela con
Avenida Principal de las Mercedes
El Rosal, Municipio Chacao
Caracas
República Bolivariana de Venezuela
Tel: 58 212 957 3403
Tel: 58 212 957 3400 (Central)
Tel: 58 212 957 3402
Tel: 58 212 957 3404
Fax: 58 212 953 0416
E-mail: presidencia@ona.gob.ve

Overall coordination, reporting to INCB and information exchange re: Table II substances.

Viet Nam

Article 18

Standing Office on Drugs and Crime(SODC)
47 Pham Van Dong Street
Tu Liem District
Ha Noi
Viet Nam
Fax: 84 4 393 87181

Article 16

Standing Office on Drugs and Crime(SODC)
47 Pham Van Dong Street
Tu Liem District
Ha Noi
Viet Nam
Fax: 844 393 87183

Article 12(*)

Director, Standing Office for Drug Control of Viet Nam (SODC)
Ministry of Public Security
No. 40 Hang Bai Street
Hoan Kiem District
Hanoi
Viet Nam
Tel: 84 694 1040 (mobile)
Tel: 84 4 3936 9893
Fax: 84 4 3938 7180
Fax: 84 4 3938 7181
E-mail: sodc.vietnam@gmail.com.vn

Wallis and Futuna Islands — Îles Wallis et Futuna — Islas Wallis y Futuna

Articles 18, 16

Direction du service de la santé
B.P. 45
Mata Utu
Îles Wallis-et-Futuna
Tel: 681 722 585

Article 12

Mission nationale de Contrôle des Précurseurs
   Chimiques (MNCPC)
Direction Générale des Enterprises (DGE)
67 rue Barbès 94201 Ivry sur Seine Cedex
France
Tel: 33 1 7984 3169
Fax: 33 1 7984 3637
E-mail: mncpc@finances.gouv.fr

Yemen — Yémen

Articles 18, 16

Supreme Board of Drugs and Medical Appliances
Ministry of Health
P.O. Box 265
Sana'a
Yemen
Tel: 967 1 252 210
Tel: 967 1 252 242-44
Fax: 967 1 251 362

Zambia — Zambie

Articles 18, 16

Ministry of Health
Pharmaceutical Regulatory Authority
P.O. Box 31890
Lusaka
Zambia
Tel: 260 211 220 429
Fax: 260 211 238 458

Article 12

Drug Enforcement Commission
P/Bag 476X, Plot No. 9347/8/9
Govt. Road, Ridgeway
Lusaka, Zambia
Tel: 260 211 255114
Tel: 260 211 255158
Fax: 260 211 254726
E-mail: commissioner@deczambia.gov.zm

Investigations of violations, controlled deliveries.

Article 12

Zambia Medicines Regulatory Authority
Plot No. 6903
Tuleteka Road/off Makishi Road
P.O. Box 31890
Lusaka, Zambia
Tel: 260 211 220429
Fax: 260 211 238458
E-mail: pharmacy@zamra.co.zm

Registration of products, licensing, inspections and issuing of import/export authorization.

Article 12(*)

The Permanent Secretary, Attn: Director of
   Pharmaceutical Services
Ministry of Health
P.O. Box 30205
Lusaka ZA 10101
Zambia
Tel: 260 1 227 745-8
Tel: 260 1 228 385-8
Fax: 260 1 222 692

Zimbabwe

Articles 18, 16

Director-General
Medicines Control Authority of Zimbabwe
P.O. Box 10559
Harare
Zimbabwe
Tel: 263 4 736 981-5
E-mail: gnmahlangu@mcaz.co.zw
E-mail: mcaz@mcaz.co.zw

Article 12

Director-General, Medicines Control Authority
P.O. Box 10559, Union Avenue
Harare
Zimbabwe
Tel: 263 4 708 255
Tel: 263 4 736 981-5
Tel: 263 4 792 165
Fax: 263 4 736 980
E-mail: mcaz@africaonline.co.zw
E-mail: gnmahlangu@mcaz.co.zw
E-mail: mcaz@africaonline.co.zw

International bodies — Organismes internationaux — Organismos internacionales

European Union (EU) — Union européenne (UE) — Unión Europea (UE)

Article 12

European Commission
Directorate-General, Taxation and Customs
  Union, Custom Policy
Rue de la Loi 200
B-1049 Brussels, Belgium

Tel.:	(32) 2-2954752
Tel.:	(32) 2-2956978
Fax:	(32) 2-2965404
Fax:	(32) 2-2964265

Competent for legislative matters and coordination of administrative cooperation. For other matters, please refer to entries for individual Member States

Inter-American Drug Abuse Control Commission/Organization of American States (CICAD/OAS) — Commission interaméricaine de lutte contre l'abus des drogues/Organisation des États américains (CICAD/OEA) — Comisión Interamericana para el Control del Abuso de Drogas/ Organización de Estados Americanos (CICAD/OEA)

Article 12

Executive Secretary CICAD/OAS
Inter-American Drug Abuse Control Commission
Organization of American States
1889 F Street, NW
Suite GSB 845H
Washington, D.C. 20006, United States of America

Tel.:	1 202 458 3178
Fax:	1 202 458 3658

International Criminal Police Organization (ICPO/INTERPOL) — Organisation internationale de police criminelle (OIPC/INTERPOL) — Organización Internacional de Policía Criminal (OIPC/INTERPOL)

Article 12

Director
Drugs Sub-Directorate
ICPO/INTERPOL
50, quai Achille Lignon
F-69006 Lyon,
France

Tel.:	33 4 72 44 70 00
Fax:	33 4 72 44 71 63

International Narcotics Control Board (INCB) — Organe international de contrôle des stupéfiants (OICS) — Junta Internacional de Fiscalización de Estupefacientes (JIFE)

Article 12

Secretary, International Narcotics Control Board
  (INCB)
Vienna International Centre
P.O. Box 500
1400 Vienna,
Austria

Tel.:	43 1 26060 4277
Fax:	43 1 26060 5868
Fax:	43 1 26060 5867
Fax:	43 1 26060 5930
E-mail:	secretariat@incb.org

World Customs Organization (WCO) — Organisation mondiale des douanes (OMD) — Organización Mundial de Aduanas (OMA)

Article 12

Director
Compliance and Facilitation Directorate
World Customs Organization
30, rue du Marché
B-1210 Brussels,
Belgium

Tel.:	32 2 209 9211
Fax:	32 2 209 9292
E-mail:	101752.3044@compuserve.com

Index of names of countries and areas

(In English alphabetical order)

Index des noms de pays et zones

(Dans l'ordre alphabétique français)

Índice de los nombres de países y zonas

(Por orden alfabético español)

www.ingramcontent.com/pod-product-compliance
Lightning Source LLC
Chambersburg PA
CBHW080848270326
41935CB00012B/1555